DON'T STALK THE
ADMISSIONS
OFFICER

DON'T STALK THE ADMISSIONS OFFICER

How to SURVIVE the College Admissions Process Without LOSING YOUR MIND

RISA LEWAK

TEN SPEED PRESS
Berkeley

For Liora and Gabriel
You can read this book in seventeen years.

Ten Speed Press and the Ten Speed Press colophon are
registered trademarks of Random House, Inc.

The student essays on pages 118–123 reprinted with permission
from the authors, Allie (essay 1) and Rebecca (essay 2).

Library of Congress Cataloging-in-Publication Data
Lewak, Risa.
   Don't stalk the admissions officer : how to survive the college admissions
process without losing your mind / Risa Lewak. — 1st ed.
       p. cm.
   Includes index.
   Summary: "A guide that helps college-bound students and their parents
navigate the college application process while maintaining their sanity and
sense of humor. Includes advice about choosing a school, writing a strong
essay, dealing with overly involved parents, preparing for standardized tests,
and more"—Provided by publisher.
1. College admission officers—United States. 2. Universities and colleges—
United States—Admission. 3. Education, Higher—Standards—United States.
4. College applications—United States. I. Title.
   LB2351.2.L49 2010
   378.1'61—dc22
                                  2010018850

ISBN 978-1-58008-060-6

Printed in the United States of America

Design by Chloe Rawlins
Cover photograph copyright © by iStockphoto.com / zxcynosure

10 9 8 7 6 5 4 3 2 1

First Edition

Contents

Acknowledgments vii

Introduction viii

PART ONE

Enjoy High School Now, Avoid Therapy Later 1

CHAPTER 1   *Overachiever* and *Loser* Have
the Same Latin Root 2

CHAPTER 2   Why Spend the Summer Meditating
with Monks When You Could Be
Working on Your Tan? 17

PART TWO

**Hot Sweats, Cold Sweats, and Difficulty
Breathing—Either You're Applying to
College or You Have Malaria** 21

CHAPTER 3   Finding the Right Fit: Why College
Isn't a Pair of Levis 22

CHAPTER 4   Guidance Counselors Must Have Done
Something Very Bad in a Former Life 39

CHAPTER 5   The SAT Versus the ACT: Which Is More Evil? . . . 54

CHAPTER 6   Surviving the College Tour:
Please God, Not Another Library 73

CHAPTER 7   When to Tell Your Parents It's Time
to Start Seeing Other Children 82

CHAPTER 8   The Art of Asking and/or Threatening
Teachers for a Good Recommendation 96

CHAPTER 9   Writing the Essay: The Line Between
Good and Bad Is Thinner Than You Think 106

CHAPTER 10   The College Interview: Fourteen Ways
Not to Screw It Up 126

CHAPTER 11   Things That Annoy Admissions Officers 136

CHAPTER 12   How to Pass the Time While
You're Waiting to Hear. 144

PART THREE
**The Envelope Arrives: Whatever Happens,
Don't Take It Out on the Mailman** 151

CHAPTER 13   Without Rejection, There'd Be
No Ben & Jerry's 152

CHAPTER 14   How to Choose the Right School
(They All Look Good in Brochures) 161

CHAPTER 15   Paying for College Without Getting Arrested . . . 170

CHAPTER 16   Taking a Gap Year: Should You Put Off
Renaissance Poetry to Explore Italy
on a Vespa?. 184

EPILOGUE   Whether It's Fat or Thin, an Envelope
Will Not Change Your Life 191

Index 194

About the Author 198

Acknowledgments

I would like to thank Kathy Green for her unwavering support and dedication to this book. I would also like to thank Ashley Thompson for all of her hard work and encouragement, and Chloe Rawlins for her terrific artistic ability.

This book wouldn't have been possible without my family's love, encouragement, and willingness to babysit. Special thanks go out to my mom, Myrna, for being a great sounding board, to my aunts Iris and Sue for their excellent feedback, and to my husband, Howard, who makes all things possible in Excel.

Finally, I want to thank all the students and parents who shared their stories with me—especially those who admitted to actually stalking an admissions officer.

Introduction

The following question won't affect your GPA:

Q: Who's happier: the overdriven, AP-inundated American high school student, or the Dayak teenager from Borneo who throws rocks at his own head during initiation rites?

A) It depends on where the Borneo kid is applying.
B) Is rock throwing weighted?
C) Ask me after November 1st.
D) What's wrong with throwing rocks at yourself?

If you answered A, then you need to chill out about the application process because you're a wee bit paranoid about your competition. If you answered B, then check with your guidance counselor, because chances are rock throwing is not offered as a course. If you answered C, then you're probably locked in your room right now calculating how many more points you need to raise your SAT score to get in early decision. If you answered D, then your parents should take you in for psychological testing.

You've spent too many nights praying that colleges will think that the summer you fed Cocoapuffs to Buddhist monks will compensate for the 0.00005839 drop in your GPA after AP Physics junior year. Your social life has gotten so bad that you're thinking about asking your SAT tutor to the prom. You can't even have normal fantasies anymore—your guidance counselor keeps showing up in a black leather bathing suit, gently rubbing your transcript with hot oil.

"Who are you, anyway?" you're asking. "I have a calculus exam tomorrow." Before you go back to Multivariable Calculus (which was actually the real cause of World War I), let me shed a little light on who I am. Basically, I am someone who feels really sorry for you—not because you're probably going to fail that Calc exam tomorrow—but because you are applying to college. Other than natural childbirth, waterboarding, and staring directly at Donald Trump's hair, very few life experiences are as painful as what you're going through right now.

I myself was once a grade-obsessed, AP-driven, SAT-defined student who rarely left the house. I spent my senior year dialing (on speed dial, of course) the University of Pennsylvania's admissions office and cajoling some poor sucker who worked the phones into answering questions like, "Has my application been read yet? I sent it priority mail. The stamp had an eagle on it—I heard the dean of admissions really likes birds. When's his birthday again?"

During that nightmare-inducing period before I got my thick envelope from Penn, I gained ten pounds (the extra chin looked swell in my senior photo), developed an obsessive tendency to write a "U" on Penn tennis balls, and began to sweat constantly. All that anxiety, angst, and armpit stains—was it worth it? Of course not. But when you're in the midst of applying to college, there is very little anyone can say or do to put things in perspective. I know for a fact that the following platitudes won't even come close to lessening your anxiety:

Life is a lot bigger than applying to college

Wherever you go, you'll be happy

There are a million good schools out there

Many CEOs of *Fortune* 500 companies went to average or below-average schools

Don't stress; it all works out in the end

You don't need a college degree to join the Mafia

I know, there are 2.6 million kids applying to college in this country and the competition is more intense now than ever before. I also understand that your parents are probably just as worried about the application process as you are. The choices are overwhelming, the application is confusing, and, let's be honest, you're waiting for an elderly relative to keel over so that the $200,000 price tag becomes less daunting.

It's easy to plunge into the depths of the hell that is college admissions (it's the unofficial tenth circle), but in truth, it's possible to put things in perspective and adopt a healthy attitude toward applying. It's even possible to get more out of high school than you think you can. And the more you can enjoy high school, the smaller your therapy bills will be later in life.

PART ONE

Enjoy High School Now, Avoid Therapy Later

High school is a time of anxiety, growth, and embarrassing breakouts. In recent years, it has also become a time of enrolling in intensive Flemish language courses, becoming a nationally ranked tennis player, defusing landmines in Africa during summer break, and maintaining straight A's—preferably by sophomore year. However, the truth is, it's unhealthy to look at high school as a boot camp for college; it's much better to devote those years to enjoying high school. By the time you've finished this section, you'll be springing out of bed at 6:00 a.m. eager to get to class and counting down the days until September during summer vacations.

CHAPTER 1

Overachiever and *Loser* Have the Same Latin Root

(This is something you may not have learned in Latin or Greek.) So, you're the poster child of overachievement: the editor-in-chief of the school newspaper, captain of the tennis team, esteemed Mathlete, member of Model Congress and Model UN, vice president of the French Club, tutor for underprivileged kids, award-winning cymbal player, and founder of JASA (Just Another Student Association). All this doesn't necessarily mean you're an accomplished person. It *does* mean you're going to run out of space on the activities grid on your application.

Extracurricular Overload

Many high school students make the mistake of thinking that the more extracurricular activities they have on their college application, the more impressed colleges will be. But before you run off to your biweekly ping pong club meeting (even *you* know that one's lame), stop and ask yourself whether you actually enjoy all these activities you're pursuing. High school is a unique time in your life to explore your interests and figure out what kind of activities, hobbies, and academic subjects *truly* appeal to you. If you dedicate your entire high school career to getting into college, you're going to squander four years of precious time running from meeting to meeting in a grim, joyless effort to appear "well rounded." Plus, you'll miss a lot of Saturday morning cartoons.

Let's be honest here: not many people join the environmental club because of a burning desire to fight human-induced climate change. The following chart outlines the alleged reason why you sign up for a particular club, and the deep, dark actual reason you joined.

Extracurricular Activity	Ostensible Reason for Joining	Real Reason for Joining
Drama Club	You live and breathe to act.	Talent is not required.
French Club	You're eager to develop language skills, which can become a lifelong asset.	You couldn't find another way to get a free trip to Paris.
Environmental Awareness Club	You think it's vital to leave our children a better planet.	The extent of your responsibility is reminding people to turn off the lights.
Yearbook	You want to contribute to your class's legacy.	The school paper wouldn't take you.
Community Service	You want to serve the underprivileged and improve your community.	You're hoping that underprivileged kid you're tutoring will wash your car.
Mathletes	You think unraveling incomprehensible, pointless math problems is fun.	You think unraveling incomprehensible, pointless math problems is fun.

If you don't really care about what you're doing, the admissions officers are going to know it. You can try all you want to pretend that working on the school paper means everything to you, but if you dread going to meetings and you write articles like "Studies Show Student Journalists Have High Suicide Rate," then your commitment to that activity will be seriously in question. You're forced to do enough things in high school; don't force yourself to attend meetings about things that don't really call out to you. You'll be doing plenty of that when you eventually get a real job.

If you're in a club that truly interests you, your commitment and dedication to that club will naturally shine through. Let's look at some specific tips for conveying your genuine passion.

Being Passionate About Your Passions

In the college admissions world, it's not enough to have passions—one must be *passionate* about those passions. Admissions officers never tire of emphasizing how important it is for students to be passionate—about anything. It doesn't matter if you like playing classical guitar or picking up dog excrement from the sidewalk. As long as you have passions and express how passionate you are about them, then you'll get a gold star in the passion department.

So remember that simply *liking* or enjoying an activity doesn't cut it anymore. If you're not zealously passionate about it, it doesn't count. There is a difference, however, between normal, run-of-the-mill passions, like playing baseball, and "we recommend intense psychotherapy" passions, like amassing a roadkill collection. Make sure your passions are within the scope of normality, and you should be fine. The following passions are not acceptable (at least on a college application).

Collecting the entire line of American Girl dolls

Throwing tea parties with imaginary friends

Anything that has to do with a boy band

Identity theft

The only way to come across as truly genuine about your activities and interests is to *be* truly genuine. You can't fake real enthusiasm. When you're writing about your passions in the essay or discussing them in the college interview, talk about how your participation in a particular activity enhances your life. Whether it's whale watching or bowling, it's easy to elaborate on something you truly love doing. If you're forcing yourself to love something, your "passion" will come across as contrived. So do what you really love—and remember that you can drop it right after you get your acceptance letter.

So how can you express your genuine passions? There are many ways, some more effective than others, as this chart demonstrates.

Good Approach	Bad Approach
Write the essay about something you are passionate about.	Write the essay about something someone else was passionate about (otherwise known as plagiarizing).
Discuss your passions in the college interview.	Mime your passions in the college interview.
Encourage your teacher to discuss your passions in the recommendation letter.	Encourage your teacher to pretend you have passions (like speaking fluent Mandarin and amassing an international cheese collection) in the recommendation letter.
Be passionate about what you truly care about it and let that come through naturally.	Buy an eccentric tweed coat and aviator sunglasses in the hope that this will make you look like an interesting, passionate person.

Do You Know What Your "Mosquito Populations and Arboviral Vectors Associated with Equines" Intel Project Means?

One tried-and-true proof of a student's passion is, of course, entering a prestigious academic competition. Among the many precollege science competitions, the Intel Science Talent Search (STS) is the country's oldest and most elite. Winners of the Intel go on to the nation's top colleges and universities, and they often have an uncanny ability to alienate everyone they meet at a frat party.

It's easy to be in awe of students who churn out this kind of research while you're still trying to figure out the difference between males and females. Don't, however, overlook one small fact: most of the Intel contestants work with an established professor who has spent years and years making strides in ground-breaking areas of research that nobody cares about. Sure, the show-offs with projects like "Mosquito populations and arboviral vectors associated with equines" can seem intimidating. However, chances are that no one, including the founder of MAA (Making America Arboviral), knows what this means.

Taking on a project like the Intel Science Talent Search is fantastic—as long as you know what you're talking about. But if you conduct any sort of research or enter a competition solely in an attempt to make yourself look good, it will backfire. Admissions officers will ask you about your research—usually by having an appropriate academic staff member from the college query you. So if you *don't* have a genuine interest in arboviral vectors, you better bone up quickly because the arboviral vector department will be getting in touch soon.

Being a Leader—Does This Mean You Can Smack People Who Don't Listen?

Admissions officers repeat ad nauseam how much they want students who are "leaders." "We want to see evidence that the student has taken charge of something and can communicate effectively," says an admissions officer from a prestigious state college in California. What does that mean, exactly? Would being the president of the debate club or vice president of the wind ensemble cut it? Or would teenage dictators of South American countries have a better shot?

Colleges' desire for students with experience in leadership roles has caused a lot of the extracurricular mania among America's high school students. Students vie for any "leadership role" to stay competitive in an admissions pool where other applicants are presenting themselves as accomplished, skilled leaders. But if everyone is a leader, then who are the followers? Why can't colleges boldly say, "Since most leaders are overrated, we're giving preference to faithful, dedicated followers"?

If you have a natural propensity for leadership and enjoy taking charge, then by all means, lead away. However, if you tend to follow the herd, then don't force yourself to be a leader. Wouldn't you rather be a genuine follower than a superficial, disingenuous leader? If being a follower allows you to participate in activities you enjoy and sleep more than three hours a night, know that you're doing yourself a service. Admissions officers prefer applicants who actually have fun doing something—even if that means you're not an officer or editor-in-chief or supreme ruler of the universe. As a former Cornell admissions officer says, "I was always more impressed with the students behind the scenes who loved what they were doing than designated leaders who were padding their resumes." There is nothing wrong with being a mere member of a club or cheering on the sidelines for your school team—those are important functions. Plus, leaders do need people to boss around and occasionally abuse, so you might come in handy.

Too Many AP Courses Can Cause Hives

"I wish my high school offered fewer AP classes," says Jenn, a junior from a private high school in New Jersey. "It would be nice to have a breather once in a while." From AP Physics to AP Lunch, the number of AP courses that are available in high school is staggering. AP classes were designed to provide students with a chance to engage in college-level coursework. The original theory was that since courses like calculus and microeconomics were already so much fun, why not take them to the next level and make them even more challenging and intense—and then top off the experience with a grueling, gut-wrenching exam in May?

AP courses do have their benefits. For starters, they go beyond the standard curriculum and elevate students' subject mastery to a new level. They offer students the opportunity to gain college credit if they receive a certain score on the exam, which could help them graduate early and save money. And last but not least, AP courses enhance a student's transcript, showing academic initiative and ambition.

Unfortunately, many students are victims of "AP mania": they feel compelled to take on lots of university-level courses because they want a competitive edge in the college applicant pool. Admissions officers state over and over that they look for students who make the most out of their high school's offerings and challenge themselves accordingly. However, too many students interpret "challenging themselves" as enrolling in as many AP's as possible—once you've taken AP Spanish and AP European History, why not add AP Chemistry, AP Studio Art,

AP Economics, and AP Calculus into the mix? The result is a masochistic course load that causes many students to experience academic overkill —not to mention breaking into hives whenever the letters "A" and "P" appear in the same word.

"I often counsel students to take the AP's they like—not the ones they think will look good on a transcript," says a guidance counselor from the suburbs of Philadelphia. "I had an excellent student of history who forced herself to take a heavy AP math and science load. She wound up doing mediocre in all subjects instead of excelling in the areas she should have." Andrew Flagel, the dean of admissions and enrollment development at George Mason University, says that "students who take five or six AP's are taking more college courses than college students. It's too much." The lesson? If you've forgotten your multiplication tables, skip AP Calculus. Ditto for AP Biology if you haven't yet figured out how babies are made.

So ask yourself whether you're a victim of AP overload. If you're not sure, here are some warning signs:

> Instead of notes, your AP American History notebook is full of deranged pictures of the founding fathers.
>
> It just hit you that those "technical institutes" advertised on TV probably don't require AP classes.
>
> You ask your AP English teacher why Shakespeare's work was never translated into English.
>
> You realized the only reason you're taking AP Bio is because you like saying the word *genitalia* out loud.
>
> You respond to every question with, "Satan trapped me."

If an honors or even a regular class appeals to you, consider taking it—even if it means setting aside your compulsion to keep up with the overachievers. It won't count as much toward your weighted GPA, but there are many other valuable benefits: you'll likely experience fewer breakdowns, stay on top of your coursework, get much more sleep, and keep your sanity intact. Plus you'll be able to shop at the A&P without having a panic attack.

Embrace Electives

Many high schools across the country are incorporating electives into the curriculum that may not appear as meaty as a typical AP class but are important in terms of rounding out your educational experience. Admissions officers are encouraging students to take elective classes because this demonstrates an openness to going beyond the normal scope of the curriculum. For your own sanity and mental health, it's a smart move to break up a heavy honors and AP course load with some less rigorous classes. So don't hesitate to take that jewelry-making or woodworking course.

Of course there are times when you wish you could design your own electives. Here's a list of electives that would actually be worth taking. One day, if you become the Secretary of Education, you could standardize them as part of high school curriculums.

Standard Electives	Interesting Electives
Topics in Modern Psychology	Coping with Your Attraction to Lunch Ladies
Technology in the 21st Century	Hack into the Registrar's Computer with Your iPhone
Public Speaking	Stop Babbling Already
Personal Finance	Take Advantage of Granny's Dementia to Get into Her Bank Account
Military History	Winston Churchill: Visionary, Leader, and Fat-Ass
3-D Animation	Analyzing Cartoons While Wasted

Charity Might Get You into Heaven But Not into Harvard

It's fantastic to want to give back to your community. It's very laudable to think of someone beyond yourself. But let's be honest: are you handing out towels to immigrants who swam here from Guatemala because you sympathize with their struggle or because you're hoping an admissions officer will view you as a caring individual? If you are truly passionate about defusing land mines in Africa, then by all means follow your bliss. But don't traipse around the African continent saying to yourself, "This will definitely make me look like a good person." If you have that attitude, it will come across in your application.

Give back to your community, but give back on your terms—not based on any preconceived notions of what the colleges want. Your time is limited, so you might have to scale back your ambitions to stay in line with reality. For instance, don't expect to help the Hondurans overthrow their dictator during your spring break. Doing something small that means something to you—even if it seems trivial in the greater scheme of things—is far more significant than trying to give back on a larger scale because you think you have to.

One student from Oceanside, New York, raised money in an effort to save a local business that had been part of the community for decades. Another student, from Orlando, Florida, read to second graders at an after-school day care center. Kelly, a student from Manhattan, visited nursing homes to apply makeup to senior citizens, which boosted their self-confidence (she went lighter on the men than on the women).

If you don't have the inclination or time to give back through community service, that's okay. Really. You can always do small things to make a difference in your immediate surroundings— set the table for dinner, take out the garbage, hold the door for someone, not run over a pedestrian when you're late for school, and so on. If you view charity as merely an extracurricular activity, colleges won't be impressed. But an attitude of real concern and compassion will come across in your essay and interview and help you in the admissions process.

Grade Grubbers Have Sold Their Souls

There are definitely things in life worth begging for: a new car, a trip to Spain, and maybe a kidney. Two extra points on a high school chemistry quiz don't even come close. So why do many of today's students beg, plead, and bribe their teachers to grant them an extra point or two on their essays and exams?

Ricky, a high school senior from Long Island, New York, tried several different methods to convince his English teacher to raise the B– he had received on a paper. First, he brought him a chocolate muffin; when that didn't work, Ricky talked to him after school. When his teacher still refused to increase his grade, Ricky took serious action. He had his aunt, who is an English teacher at a different high school, read and grade the paper. His aunt, of course, gave the paper an A. Ricky presented his aunt's feedback to his teacher, who was so annoyed that he threatened to lower the B–. Defeated, Ricky finally let it go.

While some students, like Ricky, display unrelenting tenacity, others actually get violent. Alex from New Jersey received an 88 on an AP Biology exam; when his teacher said she wasn't giving him any more points, he became so infuriated that he threw her coffee thermos onto the floor. The thermos broke, and Alex was so embarrassed and ashamed that he bought her a new thermos the next day. And then served a week in detention.

Why would anyone get so worked up and lose it like that? "Sometimes the difference between an A– and a B+ is huge," explains Laura, a high school senior from Maryland. "Acceptance can all come down to a couple of points." In today's ultracompetitive atmosphere, students are forced to be fiercely protective of every single point. After all, a 0.00087 difference between your GPA and someone else's can push you out of the Top 10, so you may feel justified in getting on your hands and knees to beg your history teacher for an extra point on your Napoleon essay because you mentioned that he was short.

Many educators believe that grade grubbing is a by-product of the hypercompetitiveness that characterizes college admissions today. Although this is true, part of the grade-grubbing epidemic stems from the inherent nature of schools' evaluation systems. Because learning is assigned a value in the form of grades, students don't have the luxury of learning for learning's sake. Grades are the constant ostensible measure of how well students have digested the material. Thus grades, not learning itself, become the ultimate goal for which everything else is sacrificed.

"There are some instances where a student has a valid case and I will raise the score," says a social studies teacher from a competitive public high school in New York City. But the teacher goes on to say that most students try and "squeeze" him for every last possible point. Eradicating class rankings has not done much to reduce grade grubbing. "It's become a game—*how far can I go and push this teacher to the limit?*" says one principal from a Long Island school district.

Remind yourself that a 96 rather than a 94 on your European History test will not make any real difference in your life. Trust me, years later you'll remember making a fool of yourself harassing your teacher much more vividly than how many points you earned for your efforts.

Here are the main things to remember about grade grubbing:

✔ Fighting for every possible point is missing the point. Learning is an end in its own right, not simply a means to a good grade.

✔ Your work and intelligence are not measured directly by the grades you receive.

✔ The time and energy you spend on grade grubbing could be much better used doing something productive or enjoyable.

✔ If you're known as a grade grubber, you run the risk of antagonizing the people you may need to write your recommendations. If you're constantly pestering your teachers to raise your grades, this will seriously affect how they view you—and a negative impression will undoubtedly come across in their recommendation letter.

✔ Grade grubbing goes on your permanent record.

Of course, there may be times when you are justified in fighting for those extra few points, but remember to pick your battles. If you don't have a strong case, let it go. Teachers don't enjoy arguing with you about points, especially if your argument is on the flimsy side. "When students reach for air for the sake of a point or two, I'm not usually inclined to raise the grade," says a teacher from New York City. "They have to really think about their arguments to convince me." A retired social studies teacher from Pennsylvania told me that he spent hours arguing with students about their test scores. He describes grade grubbing as the worst part of his job: "It was even worse than the food in the faculty cafeteria," he says. Remember that teachers are not lawyers—they don't get paid to argue.

Stick with That Sport—Even If You Were Voted Most Improved Player

No matter how many times you strike out on the baseball field or kick the soccer ball into your own team's goal, being on a high school sports team can be a truly awesome experience. Whether it's the varsity, junior varsity, or the intramural (spastic) league, playing on a team is not only a pick-me-up for your overstressed, enjoyment-starved self, but also a great exercise in discipline, commitment, and teamwork.

There is something very special about working with your peers toward a common goal, even if that goal is to grab a stick from someone and then run. Now is the time to play a sport—before you realize you're not good enough to be recruited by college coaches. If you enjoy yourself, you can participate in your college's intramural league, composed of those who were chosen last in gym class. Remember: you don't have to be good to be an athlete—you just have to look hot in the uniform.

Although it's great to be an athlete, resist the temptation to take your athleticism to an extreme. For instance, you don't have to be on the softball, soccer, *and* volleyball teams to prove you love sports. Pick and choose whatever you get the most pleasure from and focus on that sport. Aside from stressing you out, being on too many teams can be potentially detrimental in the long term if you're a serious athlete. Bryan, a college student from California, played on his high school's tennis, basketball, and baseball teams. He was an exceptionally talented baseball pitcher, but chose to play the other two sports in the off-season rather than focusing on his natural talent. "I probably could have made my college baseball team if I had devoted more time to baseball," he says. "Instead, I ended up being good at three sports rather than truly amazing at one."

Not sure which sport you'd like to pursue? There are many pros and cons to each; the chart below lists a few of them.

Sport	Pro	Con
Badminton	You improve your hand-eye coordination.	No one plays it in real life.
Soccer	You learn the importance of being a team player.	Hitting yourself on the head with a big ball is stupid.
Field Hockey	It's one of the few times in life when you're allowed to run around with a big stick.	When chasing after the ball, you realize you have the same goal as most dogs.
Track	You'll embark on an athletic activity you can do for a lifetime.	In twenty years, you'll be too tired to even look for your sneakers.
Football	You've got the whole school rooting for you.	You may not know how to read.
Basketball	You'll get into great shape fast and learn the value of strategizing.	One day you'll be shooting hoops in your driveway while the neighborhood kids taunt you.
Baseball	You're participating in one of America's finest, homegrown athletic traditions.	The uniform makes you look dumpy no matter how thin you are.

There's no avoiding it: high school is still going to suck. But hopefully this chapter will help you reap some of the benefits of your high school experience. Until there's a cure for back acne and trigonometry is eliminated from the curriculum, you'll just have to make the best of these four years.

CHAPTER 2

Why Spend the Summer Meditating with Monks When You Could Be Working on Your Tan?

The thing about Tibetan monks is that they're not exactly party animals. Unless you consider two months of fasting and limiting your vocabulary to the word *ohm* fun, you're not going to have a good summer. Yet from meditating at Himalayan monasteries to crunching numbers at math camp to charting AIDS outbreaks in Africa, high school students are desperate to show admissions officers just how dedicated they are. Gone are the days of lying on the beach every day for two months; today's students believe they must spend the summer doing something groundbreaking or innovative in order to impress colleges.

Don't Throw Away Your Summer

But what's the point of summer if you can't have fun? Forcing yourself to participate in a community service program is pointless unless you truly have a hankering to build latrines in Ghana. Summers are precious; do not throw them away by spending

July and August grimly doing something only because you believe it will give you an edge for college.

"I wanted to go to an Ivy League school, but I didn't want to give up my summer job of lifeguarding at the beach," says James, a college freshman from Atlantic Beach, New York. While all of James's friends were off studying at Harvard's summer program or slaving away as unpaid interns in a stuffy office, James sat on a tall chair all day and watched the ocean (unless someone was drowning). He spent his summers doing a job he loved and was still admitted to several prestigious universities. "I don't think my lifeguarding affected my admissions chances at all," he says. Some of James's friends who thought they were doing the right thing for the summer by traveling or attending science camp did not get into their first-choice school.

Although it's not a good idea to spend the entire summer catching up on *The Bold and the Beautiful*, you are allowed to have some fun. Take advantage of the time now, before you actually have to do something useful during your college summers to get a job after graduation. Doing something you don't enjoy will not only ruin your summer but also potentially have other negative effects.

Alex, a college sophomore from Mill Valley, California, got a summer internship at a prestigious, high-profile investment banking company in hopes that it would enhance her application. "I hated it," she admits. "I spent the entire day doing lame, menial tasks and was isolated in a cubicle. I got really depressed—even outside of work." Once her college interview rolled around, Alex struggled to explain what she had gained from the experience. "I had rehearsed a list of reasons why the job was meaningful, but my interviewer totally knew I was faking. He gave me a sympathetic smile and asked, 'Was it that bad?'" Don't be lured by the prestige of a summer program or internship if you don't have a genuine interest in what you'll be doing. Partaking in a summer activity solely for the sake of your application will inevitably work against you. Like Alex, you'll likely have difficulty being enthusiastic in your essay and interview.

Admissions officers from around the country emphasize that it's not necessary to do something monumental in terms of learning or community service in order to impress a college. An admissions officer from New York University says, "Students who work at Baskin-Robbins are just as interesting to me as students who go on summer programs in Nepal." A former admissions officer from Columbia University adds, "I didn't care what the student did for the summer—as long as it was productive."

One student from Long Island, New York, spent her summer doing a "Mitzvah Tour" up and down the East Coast. An accomplished violin player, Sara wanted to devote her talent to helping people, so she visited nursing homes to play klezmer music for the residents. Sara found the experience "completely gratifying" and had the "summer of her life," lifting the spirits of the elderly through music. "I will never forget a woman who came up to me after a performance," she says. "She remembered that her mother used to sing her one of the songs over seventy years ago. She thanked me over and over for playing that song."

Think Before It Hits 90 Degrees

Don't be like Harold from Long Branch, New Jersey, who "put no thought" into his summer plans and scrambled for a job at the last minute. Harold wound up spending his summer working at the local movie theater, sitting in a booth all day and selling "sometimes two tickets in five hours," bored out of his mind. He learned an important lesson: "I should have planned ahead. I thought something would just come to me, but I ended up having a crappy summer."

When you plan your summer activity, think about local connections. For instance, I know an aspiring journalist who asked someone at her synagogue to introduce her to the editor of the local paper. She had a great summer and gained valuable journalism experience. Another student, who is thinking about becoming a chef, asked to work in the kitchen of a luncheonette in his neighborhood. He loved the experience and had the freedom to experiment with making a crème brûlée (which is now on the menu).

Summer is a good time to try out a future career—whether it's working at a brokerage company or interning at MTV. You might be exploited labor, but at least you'll have something more substantial to put on your resume than "ate Lucky Charms and slept until noon."

Take time to carefully think about how you would *really* like to spend your summer; try to put all thoughts of college aside. Then take your college applications into consideration and figure out how your summer activity could fit in. Try to strike a balance between the two. You don't want to spend your entire summer devouring *US Weekly*, but you don't want to be imprisoned in a lifeless office doing something you detest, either. Think of something you enjoy, do some research to explore your options, and everything will fall into place.

PART TWO

Hot Sweats, Cold Sweats, and Difficulty Breathing— Either You're Applying to College or You Have Malaria

This section covers the nitty-gritty journey of college admissions. From dealing with your guidance counselor, to touring colleges that interest you, to writing the essay, to surviving the interview, you'll become more knowledgeable about the college application process and attain a deeper understanding of how frustrating and nonsensical it really is.

Although getting into college is a brutal rite of passage, it becomes much more bearable if you can take a step back and laugh at the absurdity of the admissions process. I'm currently one of two people in the country who see the humor in college admissions, but hopefully after reading this, you'll realize that the whole thing is pretty funny. Either that, or you'll collapse from nervous exhaustion, check into a psychiatric hospital, and spend the rest of your life muttering, "The creamed corn was tasty last night."

CHAPTER 3

Finding the Right Fit: Why College Isn't a Pair of Levis

There are certain things that fit just right: a great pair of jeans, a new retainer, and, hopefully, your underwear. But what about a college? Everyone talks about how vital it is to find the school that's the "right fit" for you. This is a dangerous term, however, because no single college is going to fit every aspect of your personality. And what if you have an annoying personality? Do you want to wind up at an annoying college?

The best way to begin the college search is to be honest with yourself. Will you get homesick if you go to a school far from home? Are you drawn to a particular college because everyone says you should go there or because your gut tells you it's where you belong? There are many factors that will shape your college experience, and most of them are impossible to predict beforehand: the people you'll meet, the relationships you'll develop with your professors, the age of the meat in the cafeteria (if it's green, that's a bad sign). There's no way to determine where you'll be completely happy, but there are questions you can ask yourself that will help you zero in on the schools likely to be a good "fit" (sorry, I had to use that word).

Quiz: Finding the College That Fits You Best

The following questions are designed to get you thinking about what kinds of schools you may want to attend. Your guidance counselor has probably made you fill out a similar questionnaire already, but I promise these questions won't have the same effect as your biology teacher explaining what a polypeptide is.

1. How far do you want to be from your family?

   A) A plane ride away.

   B) A train ride away.

   C) Within driving distance.

   D) I want to be home-schooled for college.

2. What is your ideal campus?

   A) Bucolic, with a chance of seeing a bear outside the dorm window.

   B) Urban, where a heavy police presence is part of the scenery.

   C) Classic, with Gothic architecture and a disturbing number of gargoyles.

   D) Institutional, with lots of concrete and a modern feel.

3. What is your desired school size?

   A) So small that I run into my professors in the bathroom.

   B) Medium, so if I break up with someone there are other people to date.

   C) Large—I like seeing between ten and twenty thousand people squeezed into a few quads.

   D) Extremely large—I want my college to be the size of a small country.

4. What kind of school would you like to attend?

    A) A career-focused school, so I won't have to sleep on the streets after I graduate.

    B) A liberal arts school, because I don't care about a job after college.

    C) Ideally, one that has both a liberal arts and a professional curriculum.

    D) Whatever, as long as I can major in human sexuality.

5. In terms of the environment, what appeals to you most?

    A) A balance between academic rigor and a healthy social life (lots of parties and nightlife).

    B) An intense, intellectually stimulating academic environment both in and out of the classroom.

    C) A challenging academic environment combined with a laidback, outdoorsy atmosphere.

    D) I'm hoping the school's mascot is a beer can.

6. How important is the prestige of a college to you?

    A) It's not important to me, but it is to my parents.

    B) I'd be embarrassed if I didn't go to a name-brand school.

    C) As long as I receive a good education, it doesn't matter.

    D) If the bumper sticker doesn't impress the driver behind me, it's not a real school.

7. Are you considering a single-sex school?

    A) Yes, because I would thrive in that environment.

    B) No, because I'm looking forward to meeting all kinds of people and don't want a limited pool.

    C) Yes, because I feel more comfortable with people of my own gender, but I'd like the option to take coed classes at an affiliated school.

    D) Does that mean you can have sex only once?

8. Are you interested in attending a religiously affiliated school?

   A) Yes, because religion is a big part of my life.

   B) Probably not, because I'm not a religious person.

   C) No, I don't want to go to a religiously affiliated school.

   D) I'm fine with any school that supports the religion of kegism.

9. Is cost a major factor in choosing a college?

   A) No; I will be able to attend college without taking out any loans.

   B) Yes; my parents can't cover the prohibitive tuition, so I need to look into student loans.

   C) Yes; private tuition is too expensive. State schools are a good option for me.

   D) Yes, unless there's a scholarship for watching animals mate on YouTube.

It's important to give these questions some serious thought, so you don't settle for a college that doesn't feel right to you. Shari, a lawyer in her mid-twenties from New York City, went to Harvard for the wrong reasons: "I got in and I thought I should go. I kind of knew that I would have been happier at another school, but you can't turn down Harvard." Shari entered the school with big dreams of becoming a world-renowned chemist. But before long, feeling alienated and lost in the massive lecture halls of chemistry and physics, she decided to major in prelaw; now she's a tax attorney. She happens to enjoy tax law, but she still wonders whether she might have explored more stimulating career opportunities had she not been so overwhelmed at Harvard.

So for those of you who think a brand-name school holds the key to an exciting, promising career, just remember Title 26,

Subtitle D, Chapter 35, Subchapter C, Section 4422 of the tax code: "*The payment of any tax imposed by this chapter with respect to any activity shall not exempt any person from any penalty provided by a Law of the United States or of any State for engaging in the same activity, nor shall the payment of any such tax prohibit any State for placing a tax on the same activity for State or other purposes.*" And that's the CliffsNotes version.

That's one Harvard casualty. Compare her with Jenna, an East Coast native and recent college grad who works as a paralegal at a big Philadelphia law firm and pursues her passion of film-making on the side. She was considering going to film school in California but knew that she was too attached to her family to attend college three thousand miles away from home. So she chose Villanova, a college located twenty minutes from her house, and she majored in communication, which offered film classes. Villanova doesn't have a film studies program, but for Jenna the trade-off was worth it. "I would have been miserable at one of the best film schools in the country," she says. "A smaller selection of film courses was worth being close to my family." Jenna prioritized what was important to her and made a decision based on what felt right. Incidentally, she visited California during one of her spring breaks and found out that she hated palm trees.

In a polar opposite case, Edward from South Brunswick, New Jersey, was dying to get away from his family and the type of people who went to his high school. He decided to attend Kent State University in Ohio, whose laidback, open-minded student body bore very little resemblance to his high school classmates. Edward, now a sophomore, says, "Going to Kent State was definitely the right decision for me. Everyone told me not to go—that there are great state schools in New Jersey—but I knew this was my chance to do something different."

If you're attached to your family and your Little Mermaid sheets, don't be afraid to factor that into your college choice. If, on the other hand, you've been waiting for eighteen years to run away from home, and college is your chance to escape, that's fine too. As long as your decision is based on *your* needs, interests, and priorities, your college choice will most likely be the right one.

If Cost Is an Issue

If the cost of tuition will play a major role in determining where you apply and ultimately enroll, consider the following financially savvy options.

✔ **Do some research before you apply.** Visit www .finaid.org/calculators to figure out how much financial aid you'll likely receive from a particular college. Calculating your EFC (expected family contribution) in advance will give you a general idea of what to expect in the financial aid package.

✔ **Go abroad.** Instead of shelling out over $50,000 a year at American institutions for eight or nine classes and a few frat parties, you can go to University College Dublin, the University of Melbourne, or the Hebrew University of Jerusalem for a fraction of the cost. Of course, going abroad for college is not for everybody. But if you have a sense of adventure, a desire to save money, or a reason to run from the police, consider spending your college years in another country.

✔ **Try community college.** Check out pages 35–38 for more info.

Quiz: Who Are You?

I'm not asking this in an existential, let's-get-to-the-root-of-your-soul kind of way—I just want to know what you'd do at a frat party. Reflecting on your traits and tendencies will help you choose a school that complements your personality. The following questions are designed to get you thinking more deeply about your future in college.

1. If you were at a fraternity party, what would you be doing?

   A) Standing against the wall and hoping that some one would approach me.

   B) Talking to the friends I came with, but that's probably it.

   C) Talking to new people and making new friends.

   D) Whatever it takes to be the life of the party— even if it means jumping on a table and screaming, "I am Zulu, lord of the dance."

2. If you wanted to take a day trip from campus one Saturday afternoon but couldn't find anyone to go with, what would you do?

   A) Go on my own; I'm an independent person.

   B) Wait for another time when my friends could come.

   C) Go by myself but spend the entire time feeling lonely.

   D) Make new friends who actually want to do something with me.

3. All of your close friends from high school are attending colleges far from you. This makes you feel:

   A) Happy, because college will be an opportunity to branch out.

   B) Scared, because my high school friends are my social support and I don't know what I'll do without them.

   C) Both excited and a little nervous—I'll miss my high school buddies, but I'm looking forward to making new friends.

   D) N/A—This question doesn't apply because I don't have any friends.

4. The idea of going to college near your parents:

   A) Comforts me.

   B) Revolts me.

   C) Makes me happy, but I won't admit it.

   D) Makes me ponder applying to the University of Zimbabwe.

5. You learn best in:

   A) Small interactive classes, because I feel more comfortable participating.

   B) Large lectures, because there's less pressure to contribute.

   C) Any class with a high-quality professor.

   D) Any environment where my snoring won't bother the professor.

6. You would like to meet people who:
    A) Are similar to me in terms of religion and background.
    B) Differ from me in every aspect.
    C) If I could clone myself, I would.
    D) Range from very similar to very different.

7. You're going to college primarily for:
    A) A top-notch education, which I'll probably forget in less than ten years.
    B) A degree, so I can get a job.
    C) The rite of passage to adulthood.
    D) The chance to shower in a coed bathroom.

When selecting a college, don't feel obligated to choose a school that seems to directly correspond to your personality. For instance, if you're on the shy side, that doesn't necessarily mean you should attend a quiet liberal arts school in the middle of nowhere. Maybe you have an urge to branch out and go to a huge state school with fifty thousand undergraduates and frat parties every night. Or if you are the most popular senior on campus, that doesn't mean you need to enroll in the state school that 75 percent of your graduating class will attend. Maybe you crave some distance from your high school buddies to see how you fare on your own.

As Polonius says in Shakespeare's *Hamlet*, "To thine own self be true." I know you're thinking, "Shut up, Polonius"—but the guy does have a point. The more you get to know yourself, the better you'll be able to determine where to apply and eventually go. You think BC Calculus is hard? That's nothing. Try being honest with yourself.

What to Do When You Have No Idea Where to Apply

When I go to college fairs, the most common question I'm asked is, "Where do you think I should apply?" I'm flattered that people wait a whole minute to get to know me before asking my advice about one of the most important decisions they'll ever make. Although college choice is not a life-and-death decision, it is certainly a big one, and there's nothing wrong with having no predetermined idea where you want to go. Sure, you might feel a little behind your best friend, who knows she wants to be a biophysics major and then attend a seven year Ph.D. program, while you can't remember whether we breathe in oxygen or carbon dioxide. The following tips will help you come a little closer to deciding where to apply when the only thing you've filled out on the Common Application is your name:

- ✔ Do not think about college rank, tier, or anything quantified by *U.S. News and World Report*. Forget about status. Remember that the Ivy League was originally formed because Cornell had an inferiority complex. Whether you want to shoot for the stars or apply to a school in a "lower" tier, don't be afraid to do so.

- ✔ Spend a weekend at a college that you or your parents think is totally wrong for you. Shattering preconceived notions about certain schools may be the first step in broadening your thinking. The college where you thought you'd be miserable may be the perfect choice.

- ✔ Think about what you might want to study in college. If it's Catholic theology, you might not want to go to Yeshiva University. You don't have to know exactly what subjects you'd like to pursue, but having a general idea should help you discover some possibilities.

✔ Picture yourself in a region of the country you've always wanted to live in, and research colleges there. I know a student from the West Coast who had no idea where she wanted to go to school but always wanted to live in the Washington, DC/Baltimore area. She found out about a place called Goucher. Once she realized that Goucher was a liberal arts college in Baltimore and not a hereditary disease, she checked it out and is now a happy junior.

✔ If you're still undecided, accept it. Don't pressure yourself into applying to a bunch of schools that aren't right for you. If it's December 31st and you still haven't figured out where to apply, then maybe it's a sign that you're not ready to go to college next September. Either that, or you're on the five-year high school plan.

Remember What's Important to You

Imagine yourself in the following scenario: You're at a college with a great football team, Jacuzzis in the bathrooms, weekly maid service, an awesome party scene, and no Parents' Weekend. Okay, so most of your classes have a hundred or more students and you can't access your professors as much as you'd like, but who cares? There are free massages every Friday in the library!

Now put yourself in this scenario: You're attending a college that doesn't have state-of-the-art facilities and has sports teams so bad they're recruiting at Little League games. But the percentage of students employed or enrolled in a graduate program within a year after graduation is high, and the student-to-faculty ratio is low. You're not that concerned about the lukewarm party scene because you're making friends and learning so much that going out on a Tuesday night isn't as enticing as you thought it would be.

Your guidance counselor would probably say that the second scenario is better because you're not supposed to consider factors like the success of sports teams, the condition of dorm rooms, and the likelihood of getting into bars with a fake ID. You're supposed to place a higher priority on factors like professor accessibility and learning outcomes. But the truth is, there is no wrong choice as long as you've taken the time to weigh which factors and attributes are important to *you*. You may decide it's more important for your school to have great facilities than a high graduate employment rate. You may decide that a killer football team is more essential for you than a small class size, and that the pleasure you'll get from painting your body every Saturday will more than make up for the lack of intimacy at a school with forty thousand undergraduates. Whatever college you choose, there will be a trade-off. No one school will embody everything you want and need, so you have to make choices.

Tara, a recent high school graduate from Texas, based her college decision on the condition of the toilets. "I knew that a really nice dorm was important to me. Every college I saw had crappy bathrooms that I would never use," she says. When Tara toured a state college in Arizona, she was in toilet heaven. "Not only were the dorms like luxury apartment buildings, but the toilets were so clean I could see my reflection. I knew I could go to a more academically selective school, but my living arrangements are really, really important to me." Tara's parents, friends, guidance counselor, and even the homeless guy down the street urged her to attend a more prestigious school. But her preference for luxurious living accommodations helped Tara decide that a state-of-the-art dorm was more vital than a higher ranking in *U.S. News and World Report*.

The only voice that's important in the college decision making is your own. You may not have multiple personality disorder, but you still have dozens of voices swirling in your head: those of your friends, parents, admissions officers, guidance counselors, and so on. Isolate your own feelings and make the best decision you can. In the end, *you* will be the one attending that college for the next four years.

Be wary of the dangerous art of "collegese," defined as "any verbal or written attempt by an admissions officer or other college representative to persuade, cajole, or entice an unsuspecting high school student to attend a particular college." Do not feel pressured to apply to or enroll in school because of an admissions officer's smooth rhetoric and slick marketing literature. To help you stay true to yourself and make sense of what admissions officers are saying, here is a handy chart that translates "collegese" into reality.

Collegese	Actual Meaning
We're continually striving to improve our student diversity.	We force the cafeteria workers to pose as students for the brochures.
Legacies are given a slight admissions advantage.	Stupid spawn have to go somewhere.
There's a strong marching band.	Cool kids don't come here.
We want a well-rounded freshman class.	We don't give a damn whether you play the zither as long as you donate after graduation.
If you work hard, you'll do well here.	Our professors get a high from failing random students.
We're located a few miles from skiing.	There's a small chance you'll die from frostbite.
We're proud to be an all-women's college.	Girls will continue to refer to the male organ as a *winky* for the next four years.

Collegese	Actual Meaning
Most students major in liberal arts.	We're banking on your not getting a job after graduation and staying here for grad school.
We encourage students to design their own major.	Your parents would be better off getting change for $200,000 and playing the Vegas slot machines.
Students take their studies seriously.	You'll have wait until after you graduate to have your first sexual experience.
Our study abroad programs add an enriching and challenging dimension to your college education.	You'll get a semester's worth of credit for sunbathing on nude beaches.

Keep in mind that two things in life are always reversible: vasectomies and where you go to college. If you're not happy at a college after a year or two, you can always transfer. As for vasectomies, you're on your own.

Community College: Why It May Be the Best Two Years You Ever Spend

Community colleges are like the beautiful, shy girl no one asks to the prom. She's totally underappreciated, has a tremendous amount to offer, and can show you a good time at a pretty cheap price. Okay, so maybe the analogy doesn't work for you, but the truth is that community colleges are becoming an increasingly popular and desirable option for college-bound students for a number of reasons:

✔ **Price:** The cost is much cheaper than that of a four-year school, so you'll actually be able buy food once in awhile.

✔ **Location:** If you're not ready to move far away from home, community colleges are a great way to branch out yet still be near your family.

✔ **Transition period:** Community colleges are an excellent way to ease into college life.

✔ **Smaller classes:** Chances are you'll get more individualized attention in the classroom.

✔ **Clean slate:** If your grades weren't as high as you would have liked in high school, community colleges are a great place to start fresh.

✔ **Gateway school:** Community college students have a higher chance of getting into four-year schools than transfer students. Many community colleges have "articulation agreements"—guaranteed admissions programs with four-year schools.

✔ **Specialized study:** Community colleges offer specialized vocational programs in dentistry, sonography, EMT, nursing, and other fields that you won't find at four-year schools.

✔ **Less pressure:** The open admissions policy of community colleges will save you the stress, heartache, and pain of filling out the Common Application. You'll sleep better at night.

Lisa, a graduate of Columbia University, decided to go to community college to fulfill her core requirements. "It just seemed like a smart way to get my core classes out of the way by spending one third the price," she says. Lisa's stellar academic performance prompted her to apply to Columbia, a school she never would have considered in high school. "No way did I have the grades for Columbia in high school. I did okay, but I was not planning on the Ivies." Lisa feels

that she was able to excel in the supportive, less pressured environment of a community college—an experience she doubts she would have had if she attended a
four-year school right out of high school.

If you have no idea what subject you want to
pursue, community colleges give you the opportunity
to decide in a low-stress, low-cost environment. "I
was totally lost in high school," says Matt, a senior at
Hunter College. He had no idea what he wanted to
study in college and was afraid of spending five or six
years at a four-year school trying to find his way. "My
math teacher said I should consider community college
because I could explore a bunch of different classes
and figure out what I liked." The strategy paid off: Matt
discovered he loved nutrition, and he is now a food science major at Hunter. "I felt totally free to take whatever I wanted, and now I'm graduating in four years,
which is a huge relief to me and my family."

Enrollment at community colleges is at an all-time
high—and it's not difficult to understand why. Students
can get a great education at the fraction of the cost and
easily transfer credits when they move on to a four-year
school. In addition, many students who have different
styles of learning or want a closer relationship with their
professors opt for the more intimate atmosphere of a
community college. "I'm a very visual person—I just
couldn't learn the way I was supposed to learn in high
school," says Olivia. "I wanted to go to college but my
grades sucked." Rather than attend a mediocre four-year
school, Olivia decided to attend a community college
for two years. "The pace was awesome and I didn't have
that panicky, behind feeling I did in high school." After
she received her associate's degree, Olivia transferred to
a fashion design school in New York City and has since
worked for top designers like Donna Karan. "Community

college saved me," she says. "I had a chance to learn at my own pace and figure out what I wanted to do instead of freaking out about passing my classes."

Community colleges give students like Olivia a second chance. So if you didn't focus in high school or just want to stay close to home to collect your weekly allowance, don't ignore a perfectly viable option. When you eventually do graduate from a four-year school, no one is going to care that you started out at a community college.

Now that you're familiar with the many pros of community college, you should know that there are a few cons as well:

The scarcity of dorms means you'll still have to make out in your car.

The bumper sticker looks stupid when you cross out the words "community college" with a black permanent marker.

You can say you're an evil genius who finished college in two years, but no one will believe you.

You may be recruited for the football team even if you've never touched a football.

The cafeteria consists mainly of vending machines.

Because of the flexible class schedules, you may have to dissect Shakespearean sonnets at 2 a.m.

Your classmates will be from all walks of life: working mothers, fifty-year-old cab drivers, and foreign students who hold higher degrees from their home country looking to perfect their English. In other words, you might be one of the few students who still has acne.

CHAPTER 4

Guidance Counselors Must Have Done Something Very Bad in a Former Life

Guidance counselors have one of the roughest jobs in America. Not only do they have to deal with the excruciating minutiae of getting hundreds of kids into college, but they have to get up really, really early. No wonder they're cranky most of the time.

Often guidance counselors don't provide the advice or assistance you need because they're responsible for dozens—if not hundreds—of other students. In private schools in the United States, the average student to guidance counselor ratio is 60 to 1. Public school students get far less personal attention, with a staggering ratio of 315 to 1. "It's not our fault," says Sue, a guidance counselor at a large public high school in North Carolina. "We have so many other things to deal with—students' family issues, behavioral issues—that a lot of times college isn't at the top of our list of priorities."

Because guidance counselors do have a lot on their plate— from helping families attain standardized test waivers to taking really long lunches—you may find that, unfortunately, your guidance counselor doesn't know you well at all. "My guidance counselor knew my name, but that was about it," says Paul, a high school senior from the suburbs of Boston. "During my junior year meeting to talk about colleges, his eyes were studying my transcript the entire time. It was like he was cramming to learn who I was."

Fend for Yourself

Whether you attend a public or private school, the best thing you can do for yourself is to become your own guidance counselor. If you rely solely on your guidance counselor for the support, information, and expertise you need during the college admissions process, you will be putting yourself at a serious disadvantage. There are several reasons why you should fend for yourself:

1. Your guidance counselor doesn't care about you.

2. Unless you have a prison record, you won't meet with your guidance counselor that frequently before your junior year.

3. Your guidance counselor recommends the same twenty-five schools to everyone.

It is imperative to do your own research when it comes to the college search. Lara, a college graduate from a state school in New York, says that her guidance counselor made a serious blunder that could have profoundly affected her future. "I was dying to get into this one school that I didn't have the grades for. I asked my guidance counselor if there were any special programs or scholarships that I could apply for, and she said no." By taking her guidance counselor's word for it, Lara resigned herself to going to a community college close to home and being "absolutely miserable." On a whim, Lara's mother called her reach school to double-check about special programs. It turned out that the school did have a "Special Student" program that catered to below-average students with unique abilities—which in Lara's case was writing.

Lara applied and got in. "I thank my mom every day for making that call," she says. Lara's mother was smart enough to know that her daughter's guidance counselor hadn't done a thorough job. Even guidance counselors with the best of intentions cannot possibly know every aspect of every school, and very often they don't have the time to make inquiries on your behalf. So do yourself a favor and keep the following hints in mind:

> Don't take what your guidance counselor says as gospel. If she says, "You can't get into Harvard—you're a cretin," apply anyway—even if you are a cretin.
>
> Always listen to your gut instincts even if they clash with your guidance counselor's suggestions.
>
> Your guidance counselor will come up with a list of safety schools, middle-of-the-road schools, and reach schools for you. Take these with a *major* grain of salt. And then rip up the piece of paper.
>
> If your guidance counselor is clearly not connecting with you or making any real effort on your behalf, think of him as your senile grandpa. Smile, nod, tune out when he starts to babble, and ignore the request to sit on his lap.

Allison from Baltimore, Maryland, had minimal help from her guidance counselor when she was applying to film schools. Allison's guidance counselor was decent but not at all knowledgeable about her specific area of interest, and admitted she knew nothing about film programs. Rebecca, Allison's older sister, told her to reach out to current film students and alumni at the schools she was interested in. "It made all the difference," says Rebecca. "Allison found out what she needed in her applications and which schools she should focus on."

Much as you'd like your guidance counselor to be well versed in the minutiae of every single school in the country, the fact is, many guidance counselors are not knowledgeable about programs that are off the beaten track. So if you're interested in nonmainstream, specialized fields—visual arts, musical theater, fashion, film design, architecture, and so on—you'll likely have to become your own guidance counselor and pursue appropriate programs and schools on your own.

The Caring Versus the Uncaring: Know What Kind of Guidance Counselor You're Dealing With

The vast majority of guidance counselors do actually care about students, but simply don't have the time to be as devoted as they would like. However, there is a spectrum of guidance counselor involvement and concern, running from the super dedicated to those who don't care whether you live or die. Here are some clues to tell the difference.

Dedicated Guidance Counselor's Questions and Comments	Indifferent Guidance Counselor's Questions and Comments
Here's a list of 590 schools that match your exact criteria.	You look familiar . . .
What are your ultimate career goals?	Have you considered starting a Ponzi scheme as an alternative to a college education?
I proofread your essay and made several suggestions.	I noticed you spelled *college* with one L and I didn't do a damn thing.
Let's sort through the financial aid process.	Is FAFSA contagious?
What else can I do to strengthen your application?	The hell with college—go start making babies.

Your guidance counselor likely falls somewhere in between these two extremes. If you're dealing with the dedicated variety, consider yourself lucky—just be vigilant for any signs of separation anxiety in your guidance counselor once you've been accepted somewhere. If you're dealing with the indifferent type, consider investing in a private counselor (or voodoo doll).

What to Do When Your Guidance Counselor Just Doesn't Listen

"I've told my guidance counselor several times that I don't want to go to a small school far from home," says Jackie from Port Washington, New York. "For some reason, he keeps pushing this school called Franklin Pierce in New Hampshire, which is a probably a great school, but has nothing to do with what I want."

It's a familiar scenario: you tell your guidance repeatedly where you're interested in going to college and what your criteria are, and he comes up with a recommendation that's so far out of left field you have no idea where it came from. If this happens to you, you have two options:

Option A: Slap your guidance counselor in the face.

Option B: Completely ignore what he says.

Okay, assaulting a guidance counselor doesn't usually boost a student's college application, so you really have only Option B. You know what you want better than your guidance counselor does, so have the confidence to apply where you want to go. When I was exploring colleges, my guidance counselor told me not to apply early decision to the University of Pennsylvania because she thought I'd be a better fit at Bucknell. I have no idea why she connected me with Bucknell, but I knew in my heart that Penn was where I wanted to be. I disregarded her advice and had a great experience at the school where my instincts told me to apply.

When it comes to dealing with your guidance counselor, be polite but firm. Stick to your guns and stand up for yourself, even if she's pushy. Tell her that you appreciate her advice, but that you are applying to the school that feels right to *you*.

Common Exchange Between Guidance Counselor and Student

Student: I'm interested in going to a school with a warm climate and a lively social scene. I'm thinking about the University of Florida.

Guidance Counselor: You should also apply to the University of Montana.

Student: Um, okay . . .

The following week

Student: I need my transcript sent to the University of Florida.

Guidance Counselor: Have you given any thought to the University of Montana?

Student: No. I want to go to school in Florida.

Guidance Counselor: Really? Montana would be a really good fit for you . . . but all right, I'll send your transcript to the University of Florida. *Writes "Send to University of Montana" on the transcript.*

Your Parents and Your Guidance Counselor: Proceed with Caution

When it comes to the college application process, guidance counselors often find themselves caught in the middle of a tug of war between student and parent. The intense emotion, stress, and anxiety that plague you and your parents very often come to a head in the cozy confines of your guidance counselor's office. A guidance counselor at a private school in Maine says that one student screamed at her parents, "'If you had a happier marriage, I'd definitely have a higher GPA!'" A guidance counselor from New York City reports that the mother of a very competitive student collapsed in her office from nervous exhaustion.

The goal of bringing your parents and guidance counselor together is to talk about where you will go to college. Anything else is irrelevant. The meeting is not a venue for enacting family dramas, so don't turn it into an episode of *Dr. Phil*. To have a productive meeting, consider the following suggestions:

- ✔ Brief your parents in advance on everything you've been doing up to this point regarding college admissions.

- ✔ Form a unified front. Even if you were choking your mom at breakfast, don't fight in front of your guidance counselor (who probably has Family Services on speed dial).

- ✔ Ask your parents not to take what your guidance counselor says personally. Even if it's "Were you under the influence when you conceived Timmy?"

- ✔ Have your parents write a list of questions for your guidance counselor. Warn them that they most likely will not be answered.

- ✔ Wait until you've left the guidance counselor's office to beg for a private counselor.

Take Advantage of Your Guidance Department

Your school will most likely offer a "College Night" and/or "Financial Aid Night" in your junior or senior year (or both). You and your parents should take advantage of any and all college events at your school. Don't assume that you know everything about the application process and have the luxury of blowing off these gatherings. You'd be surprised at what you can learn—plus, in most cases, there's free food.

"The reason we have these evenings is to break down the college process for parents because it's so overwhelming," says Jan, an administrative assistant at a high school guidance office outside of Boston. "The students and parents who don't come to these events are usually the most stressed—they come into our office every other day in a complete panic." One guidance counselor from Connecticut recalls a parent who used the guidance office as her personal consulting firm. "She would come in at least twice a week to ask either an insignificant question or a completely inconsequential question," he says. "When I asked her whether she attended our college panel night, she just shrugged and told me there was no point because I would explain everything to her anyway."

Do Not Let This Be Your Parent

If you could imagine your mom or dad having the following exchange with your guidance counselor, then they're definitely too uninformed about the application process.

Parent: Excuse me, could I ask you a few questions about college applications?
Guidance Counselor: Sure.

Parent: How does my son apply to colleges?
Guidance Counselor: Um, he can start by filling out the Common Application.
Parent: Is that on the machine?
Guidance Counselor: Machine?
Parent: You know, the computer.
Guidance Counselor: Yes, just go to www.common application.com.
Parent: I have to visit the Interweb?
Guidance Counselor: Yes . . . you use the Internet.
Parent: Is there another way he can apply?
Guidance Counselor: Well, he can request applications from individual colleges or fill them out online. (*Pauses.*) I really have to get going.
Parent: Can I come with you? I still have a lot of questions.
Guidance Counselor: We answered a lot of basic questions at our College Night last week.
Parent: Yes, I wanted to go to that, but it conflicted with the season premiere of *Wife Swap*.
Guidance Counselor: (*Walks toward the door.*) I'm sorry, but I really have to go.
Parent: That's okay, I'll call you at home later.

Guidance counselors do not have the time to hold your hand—or your parent's hand—through every step of the admissions process. You and your parents must equip yourselves with as much information as possible, whether it's by talking to people in the know, buying books, scouring the Web, or going to college fairs and high school information nights. Your mom and dad can be powerful allies (remember Lara's mother?), so you should encourage them to be informed and inquisitive without becoming obnoxious or taking control of the college application process.

Do You Need a Private Counselor?

"If you have a good guidance counselor, you shouldn't need a private counselor," says a guidance counselor from Long Island, New York. If that's true, then why are there over five thousand private college counselors in the country? Most likely because in today's college application market, it can feel like a competitive disadvantage if you don't employ the services of a private counselor. To use the quintessential peer-pressure argument, "Everyone's doing it." So are there any major advantages to hiring a private counselor?

"Private counselors don't really do anything that guidance counselors don't do, but it makes parents feel that they're giving their child a leg up," says a high school guidance counselor who moonlights as a private counselor in a neighboring school district. This particular counselor told me that the main reason parents hire her is because they don't want to deal with their children's applications. "I literally sit at the child's computer and organize their application. I keep them on top of deadlines, bring envelopes and stamps, and tell them what they have to put in each one."

Very often, private college counselors are the liaison between parents and their children. Because the admissions process produces so much tension within a family, the private counselor functions to absorb the friction by being the "nag" the parents don't want to be. "Parents tell me all the time that their kids won't listen to them. But because I'm being paid and I'm not their parent, the kids listen to me," says Cheryl, a private counselor in the Washington, DC, area. And paid they are. In general, private counselors charge families an average of $3,700 for a package of services, with an hourly rate that ranges from $160 to $300. (It's a helluva lot more remunerative than babysitting.)

Within the world of private counseling, however, there are many different varieties: the high school guidance counselor turned private counselor, the college admissions officer turned private counselor, the just-released inmate who needs a paycheck turned private counselor, and so on. Because anyone can hang out a shingle and claim the title of private college counselor, education consultant, or educational strategist, how do you know who is legitimate? Unfortunately, you don't. Private counselors don't need to meet certain criteria or earn a license to practice, so the consumer must choose one carefully. However, there are a couple tried-and-true ways to find a good private counselor:

✔ **Word of mouth:** Talk to people who have had experience working with private counselors, such as parents who have seen them in action. A counselor's reputation is determined by recommendations from clients, so ask around.

✔ **The Independent Educational Consultants Association (IECA):** Visit www.educationalconsulting.org to locate private counselors in your area. To be an IECA member, private counselors must meet specific requirements, such as having a master's degree, working three years in counseling or admissions, and advising at least fifty students in private practice. This is a great resource for finding qualified private counselors.

Most of the parents and students I spoke with said they felt most confident with a counselor who had experience working in a college admissions office. One of the most sought-after private counselors in the country believes that being a former admissions officer gives her a huge advantage in helping students apply to the right schools. She explains that her knowledge and background enable her to get into the mind-set of an admissions committee and develop an extremely accurate idea of where a student will be accepted. "If I know they don't have a shot at Harvard, I may tell them to apply to Penn or Cornell early decision, where they stand a stronger chance," she says.

Stephen Friedfeld, a former admissions officer at Cornell and the cofounder of EqualApp, a website that offers a "virtual college counselor" and application tools, agrees. He believes that his admissions experience is especially helpful when it comes to improving students' essays. "Your teachers, parents, and guidance counselor might know what good writing is, but they may not know what good college essay admissions writing is," he says. Stephen suggests that people only hire a private counselor with prior admissions experience. "I know what the admissions committee is looking for," he says.

A private counselor provides a safety net and sense of security for students and parents in the brutal and often nonsensical process of college admissions. They are paid to be available at 10 p.m., during the summer, and over Thanksgiving break if you need them. However, don't make the mistake of believing that a private counselor possesses an entry-gaining power you don't have. Even if you have the most talented, dedicated counselor imaginable, he or she won't be able to make you a competitive applicant with a 1.8 GPA.

Taking risks is a big part of the college admissions game, and you shouldn't be afraid to do so. You need to realize, however, that private counselors will not always encourage you to take those risks; their reputations are built on their clients' acceptances, so sometimes they'll want to play it safe. The bottom line: no private counselor (or guidance counselor, for that matter) knows *exactly* how an admissions committee will respond when they review your file. It's impossible to predict how something in your application or essay will strike an admissions officer.

The moment you begin working with a private counselor, your application ceases to be solely yours. Whether you realize it or not, you are absorbing someone else's input, ideas, and energy that will subtly trickle into your application. In fact, one student from Wellington, Florida, decided not to work with a private counselor for that very reason and found that it helped her better cope with rejection. "That way, I knew they were rejecting me, not someone else's method of getting me into a school," she says. If you seek too much consultation, you run the risk of diluting your individual stamp on the application. Don't forget that the best thing about your college application is, quite simply, you.

How can you tell whether you might benefit from a private counselor?

- ✔ Your guidance counselor isn't giving you the level or amount of advice you need.
- ✔ You want a fresh pair of eyes to critique and improve your essay.
- ✔ When it comes to the college application, you need a buffer between you and your parents.
- ✔ You find the application process overwhelming and need help breaking it into manageable steps.
- ✔ You would like the insight of a former admissions officer.
- ✔ You don't know how to put paper into an envelope.

Still not sure whether to spring for a private counselor? Check out the chart for several key differences in the advice you'll receive from a guidance counselor and a private counselor.

Private Counselor's Feedback	Guidance Counselor's Feedback
Try not to be an idiot.	If you're an idiot, there's not much I can do.
Move your essay margins $1/4$ inch to the left.	Move your essay margins $1/4$ inch to the right.
Remember that you're $1/16$ black.	If you're friends with an African American, you can check the minority box.
Have you considered moving to Tehran to gain a geographic advantage?	Are there any guidance counselor openings in Tehran?
Try to have a life-changing experience by senior year so you can write about it in the essay.	Smash your head against the wall and write about overcoming brain trauma in the essay.

Online Resources to Check Out

Although you shouldn't rely solely on a website to answer all of your questions about college admissions, you can definitely use the Internet as an adjunct to your guidance counselor—much like the TAs (teaching assistants) you'll turn to in college when it's clear your professor doesn't have time for you.

Visit **College Confidential** (www.collegeconfidential.com) to get free information about every aspect of the college admissions and selection process. Admissions professionals—as well as parents and students currently going through the college application process (and those who have survived it)—answer questions on a huge range of topics, including admissions, college search, and college life.

And when you need a break from the serious stuff, visit **Admissions Angst** (www.admissionsangst.com) for fun, entertaining articles about college admissions.

CHAPTER 5

The SAT Versus the ACT: Which Is More Evil?

It's like asking "Who's worse: the Joker or Lex Luthor?" As Batman and Superman can attest, they both suck. No one, even those who get a perfect score, enjoys taking standardized tests.

Although the ACT is nightmare-inducing in its own right, there is no known man-made instrument of torture more powerful than the SAT. Throughout history, the SAT has caused people to:

A) Drop out of high school

B) Sweat like a farm animal

C) Vomit

D) Associate No. 2 pencils with the devil

E) All of the above

The only positive aspect of the SAT is that after high school, it's over. You'll never, ever have to take it again (unless you become an SAT instructor), and people will rarely ask about your score. And if someone does have the nerve to ask, you can respond with one of the following statements:

I don't remember. (You bombed the test.)

I did pretty well. (That could mean anything from a 300 to a 2350.)

I got a 2400. (You're giving yourself a 400-point curve.)

I'll tell you mine if you tell me yours. (You're going to lie anyway, so why not let this nosy jerk lie first?)

Which Test Should You Take?

Determining which test to take is really a matter of personal preference. Many students opt to take both, not because they are certifiable, but because they feel comfortable with both tests and believe that submitting two scores will enhance their application. This dual-test strategy is beneficial when both scores are high. On the other hand, if you scored in the 90th percentile on the ACT, but the only points you earned on the SAT were for writing your name, this tactic probably isn't so effective.

This comparison chart outlines the basic similarities and differences between the tests.

	ACT[1]	SAT[2]
Total time	2 hours, 55 minutes, plus optional 30-minute essay	3 hours, 5 minutes, including mandatory 25-minute essay
Frequency	Offered six times per year	Offered seven times per year
Subjects	English, Mathematics, Reading, Science, and Optional Essay	Critical Reading, Mathematics, and Writing
Organization	Sections always follow the same order	Sections are arranged randomly
Answer type	Multiple choice, except for the optional essay	Multiple choice, except for the essay and ten student-produced responses ("grid ins") in the math section

1. Official ACT website (http://www.actstudent.org/testprep/descriptions/index.html).
2. Official SAT website (http://professionals.collegeboard.com/testing/sat-reasoning/about/sections).

	ACT	SAT
Math section	Consists of pre-algebra, elementary algebra, intermediate algebra, coordinate geometry, plane geometry, and trigonometry	Consists of numerical operations, algebra and functions, geometry and measurement, and data analysis, statistics, and probability
Reading section	Consists of passages from different fields (social studies, natural sciences, prose fiction, and humanities)	Consists of passages from different fields (social studies, natural sciences, prose fiction, and humanities) and sentence completion
Science section	Consists of biology, chemistry, physics, and the Earth/space sciences	Not included
Writing section	Optional essay with one prompt	Sentence improvement, recognizing sentence errors, and improving paragraphs, plus required essay with one prompt
Section time	Required sections range from 35 to 60 minutes	Sections range from 10 to 25 minutes
Incorrect answers	No penalty for guessing; only correct answers count	Penalty for guessing; no penalty for blank responses
Conclusion	Evil	Eviler

So, which test should you take? Tim Levin, the founder and CEO of Bespoke Education, a tutoring and test prep company based in New York City, suggests that students start preparing for the SAT first. He believes that once they are comfortable with SAT strategies, it's easier to make the leap to the ACT. As you saw in the comparison chart, the ACT consists of four areas: English, Mathematics, Reading, and Science. The ACT is a curriculum-based exam that evaluates what you've learned in school so far, whereas the SAT measures general problem-solving skills and reasoning ability. If you aren't the best test taker in the world, the ACT may be the better test for you.

Tim believes that the SAT is more nuanced and less straightforward than the ACT, and for that reason it can be harder for students who aren't as adept at games and problem solving. On the other hand, because the ACT packs a lot more material into its sections, Tim says students might run out of time more quickly on the ACT than on the SAT.

Know your own strengths and weaknesses as a test taker. Do you constantly run out of time during your exams in school? Are you more comfortable with the predictable order of the ACT sections than the random organization of the SAT sections? You must weigh the pros and cons of each test and decide which one caters more to your strengths. And if you think this self-analysis is fun, you'll have a ball taking both tests—which is, unfortunately, the best way to determine which one you're naturally more comfortable with.

Although most colleges in the country accept both the SAT and ACT, their policies and preferences do vary, so be sure to check the standardized test requirements at the schools you're interested in.

A Note on Score Reporting

Because the SAT and ACT's rules on score reporting have changed a lot in recent years, it's best to check their websites for the most up-to-date information. Also be aware that score-reporting policies differ from college to college, so get the scoop on each school before sending in your scores.

Questions That Should Be on the SAT

Since you've probably seen dozens, if not hundreds, of sample SAT questions practically indistinguishable from those on the real test, I won't subject you to another round of that torture. Instead, here are the kind of questions you may find yourself fantasizing should be on the test . . .

Math Questions

1. Which triangle is the prettiest?

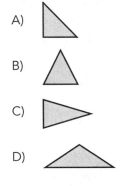

A)

B)

C)

D)

E)

2. If K is having an identity crisis and doesn't know whether it's a positive or negative integer, what would you suggest?

A) Put K in therapy.

B) Tell K to stop overanalyzing.

C) Encourage K to experiment.

D) Give K some "E."

E) Tell K to date 0 and have a codependent relationship.

3. If $f(x) = x^2 + x$, $f(3) = x^3 - y^2$, and $r = 3$, so $(r^2 - 2)(n + 1) = y^3$, what is the maximum value of a 2009 iPod sold on eBay?

    A) What the hell?

    B) You lost me after $f(x)$.

    C) Thank you for finally asking a useful question.

    D) My head hurts.

    E) x^2 can go put it where the sun don't shine.

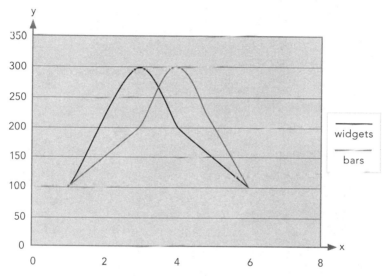

4. Which of the following explanations best describes the figure shown?

    A) A man doing something obscene.

    B) A woman doing something obscene.

    C) A hermaphrodite doing something obscene.

    D) Y and X getting it on.

    E) Y and X fantasizing about widgets and bars.

Verbal Questions

1. Even though the SAT _____, most colleges require prospective students to take it.

   A) sucks

   B) super sucks

   C) sucks to infinity

   D) would be more effective than Chinese water torture

   E) All of the above

2. When studying for the SAT, students realize it is both _____ and utterly _____.

   A) useless.......moronic

   B) horrendous.........heinous

   C) torturous........draining

   D) sickening.......deflating

   E) worse than death........makes purgatory look like a good time

3. The people who write the SAT were clearly _____ as children and are _____ their revenge on the world.

   A) social outcasts.......exacting

   B) never hugged.........plotting

   C) dropped onto hard surfaces........planning

   D) smacked........thrilled to unleash

   E) Can I destroy these people?

4. <u>The, creators of, the SAT; don't realize, how annoying, it is, to read, sentences with, commas after, every other, word.</u>

   A) We speak English, dimwits.

   B) I'm, not, sure, of, the, answer, ; : , , :" ,

   C) They can stick the commas up their &*%$.

D) The only people whose speech resembles the SAT grammar questions are in mental institutions.

E) The creators of the SAT belong in mental institutions.

The Essay

Many students think that the most frustrating and confusing part of the SAT is the essay. They observe that the questions fall into one of two camps: very vague and open-ended or very complicated and specific. The following sample prompts probably won't show up on test day, but they should give you an idea of the kind of questions that await you.

EXAMPLE 1

Some say life is really cool. Others say life is not so cool. Still others say life is a mixture of cool and uncool. What is your stance on the nature of life? Please support your position with reasoning and examples taken from your reading, studies, experiences, or observations.

EXAMPLE 2

"Man is spirit. But what is spirit? Spirit is the self. But what is the self? The self is a relation which relates itself to its own self, or it is that in the relation [which accounts for it] that the relation relates itself to its own self; the self is not the relation but [consists in the fact] that the relation relates itself to its own self. Man is a synthesis of the infinite and the finite, of the temporal and the eternal, of freedom and necessity, in short it is a synthesis. A synthesis is a relation between two factors. So regarded, man is not yet a self."

—Søren Kierkegaard, *Sickness Unto Death*[3]

Assignment: Can you tell us what the hell this means?

3. Søren Kierkegaard, *Sickness Unto Death* (Radford, Virginia: A & D Publishing, 2008), 9.

EXAMPLE 3

In *Gone with the Wind*, Rhett Butler said to Scarlett O'Hara, "Frankly, my dear, I don't give a damn." Do you think he was being a tad harsh? Explain why.

EXAMPLE 4

"*Zero-knowledge proofs* are interactive proofs with the amazing property that the verifier *learns nothing* from its interaction with the prover, other than the fact that the assertion being proven is true. Zero-knowledge proofs have vast applicability in constructing secure cryptographic protocols."
—Salil Vadhan, "Interactive Proofs & Zero-Knowledge Proofs"[4]

Assignment: Can you characterize zero-knowledge proofs and eliminate the complexity assumptions used in the study of zero knowledge?

Well, can you?

Time Is the Enemy

Wouldn't it be great if you had an entire weekend to take the SAT? You could take naps between sections, chug an espresso after a really boring reading passage, and stash a dictionary in the bathroom to look up what *inchoate* means. Unfortunately, many students have the problem of running out of time on both the SAT and the ACT. It's you against the clock. You don't have the luxury of rereading a passage or spending ten minutes on a math problem. You have to be quick and move on.

The best way to conquer the time constraint is to fake a case of ADD and get an official extension. Just kidding. The real key is to zero in on your weaknesses and work on strengthening

4. Salil Vadhan, "Interactive Proofs & Zero-Knowledge Proofs," http://people.seas.harvard.edu/~salil/areas.html (accessed May 2010).

these skills. Ed Carroll, the executive director of high school programming for the Princeton Review, says that if you want to improve your score (and your timing) on standardized tests, you need to analyze your tests and pinpoint your problem areas. If you've only taken practice tests so far, try to identify a pattern to the questions you've answered incorrectly: Are you mostly struggling with algebra? Are you guessing on a lot of the grammar questions? Do you need a crash course in vocab? If you've already taken the test, carefully examine your score report. As Ed explains, "Score reports that break down what you're getting wrong are very important"—they provide an analysis of your weaknesses and enable you to detect patterns.

Many students think that simply going through the testing experience—by taking either an actual exam or a mock exam with standard conditions (timing, environment, and protocol)—is an effective score-boosting strategy. However, if you skip the critical step of examining your problem areas, you will seriously limit your potential for progress. According to Ed, "If you're just taking the test over and over again without analyzing your weaknesses, you're not going to improve." Why? Because you aren't learning; you're performing. Once you've identified your problem areas, you can focus on them and come up with a plan of attack. Ed recommends that students practice their weak points without the constraint of a time limit, which will go a long way toward improving their performance and timing.

So rather than taking three practice SATs in a weekend, spend your time going over the questions that you are consistently getting wrong. Once you master your weaknesses, your pacing will automatically improve, and you'll have the confidence and ability to get those questions right on test day.

The Word on Test Prep

Blame it all on Stanley Kaplan, the test prep pioneer. Kaplan is the main reason students now feel compelled to take an SAT or ACT prep class. Unfortunately, because the SAT (more so than the ACT) is a strategically challenging test, the multimillion-dollar test prep industry does have some justification for its existence: the techniques they teach you can actually come in handy. Among other things, a good standardized test prep class can:

- ✔ Boost your confidence in your ability to take the test
- ✔ Suggest strategies for conquering tricky questions
- ✔ Help you pinpoint your problem areas
- ✔ Fill in some of the gaps in your education so you have a stronger knowledge base to draw from
- ✔ Provide you with the opportunity to take mock tests under actual SAT/ACT conditions
- ✔ Give you a chance to hit on new people

With the plethora (SAT word alert!) of prep classes out there, how do you choose a good one? Tim Levin suggests that students and parents ask a few crucial questions before committing to a course:

- ✔ What are the tutors' credentials? Do they have teaching experience or are they out-of-work actors who took the test once fifteen years ago?
- ✔ What is included in the test prep package? Will students receive a comprehensive experience, with regular homework, mock tests, and score reports and analysis?
- ✔ What educational materials does the company use (sample tests, study aids, specialized software, and so on) and how do they select these?

✔ What kind of training do the tutors receive? Are they using a review book you can pick up at any bookstore, or do they have proprietary material they created specifically for their courses?

✔ How small are the classes? (If you're in a room with fifteen kids, you might not be getting the attention you need.)

Do your research. You don't want to waste time and money with a useless prep class. Word of mouth is a great way to get the scoop on the effectiveness of a test prep company. (If the tutor spends the bulk of the class drinking from a bottle in a brown bag, that won't be advertised in the brochure.) Remember that no test prep company can guarantee you your target score. However, they can help you build the confidence and experience you'll need to do well. Standardized testing has a strong psychological component, so the more convinced you are of your ability to conquer the test, the more calm and sharp you'll be when you take it for real.

If you learn best one-on-one or feel that a prep class is too big, private tutoring is an excellent option. The cost could be double or even triple what you would pay for a larger class, but the benefits may be worth it. Private tutors can be especially helpful as they give you personalized attention rather than a broad, one-size-fits-all overview. For instance, if you want to improve a particular problem area, a private tutor can spend the session focusing on this weakness. Just make sure that you're comfortable with your tutor and that he or she has a good reputation (and good personal hygiene—since you won't have the buffer of a classroom).

When You Can't Afford a Prep Class

Not everyone can afford the luxury of organized test preparation (if you call spending your free time factoring polynomials a luxury). There's no doubt that prep classes are a financial burden and therefore not an option for many people. This is where the Internet comes in handy. There are a number of excellent websites that offer free or low-cost standardized test preparation. Granted, it's not the same thing as personal tutoring, but it's certainly better than praying for an arsonist to show up at your test site on SAT day.

Vocabulary Building Resources

Vocab Sushi (www.vocabsushi.com) is my favorite vocabulary-building website—and in my opinion the most effective one. The site's motto is "bitesize learning," and it makes acquiring new vocabulary words a manageable task. Vocab Sushi is unique in that it teaches you vocabulary based on context, not definition. Gone are the days of flashcards and memorization by rote—you'll learn the meaning of words by seeing them in current news articles. Another great feature is the site's adaptive learning model, which provides you with a customized list of words to master. Through quizzes, sentence completions, and other tools, you can practice using these words as the site monitors your progress. Oh, and did I mention the site is completely devoid of advertising? You can focus on learning vocabulary without the distraction of pop-up ads for Xbox.

Free Rice (www.freerice.com) actually combines a noble cause with standardized test prep. Run by a division of the United Nations, this nonprofit site has a very addictive, adaptive vocabulary test that fulfills the mutual need to acquire vocabulary and donate rice. Free Rice pledges, "For each answer you get right, we donate 10 grains of rice through the World

Food Program to help end hunger." Even though using the site doesn't count as community service, it's a great way to broaden your vocabulary and do something good for the world at the same time.

Students who are tech-savvy and time-strapped (which pretty much describes everyone these days) will appreciate **Test-wiser** (www.testwiser.com). For $25 you can download SAT-level words onto your MP3 player and learn vocabulary at your own pace. Just don't try to learn all three thousand words at once.

VerbaLearn (www.verbalearn.com) is a free site that offers customized wordlists, MP3 downloads, sentence completions, and video flashcards.

If you're a visual learner, try **GotBrainy** (www.gotbrainy .com). This free site allows users to submit pictures and videos to creatively illustrate the meaning of a word. It also features vocabulary in context, pulling sentences from great literature to reinforce words' meanings. (Sorry, Danielle Steel is not part of the "great literature" club.)

General Test Prep Resources

ePrep (www.eprep.com) charges $67 to $300 for video-based SAT or ACT preparation. Expert video instruction is available day or night on their website, and ePrep monitors your progress.

Number2 (www.number2.com) is a free website that offers customized online SAT and ACT prep courses, which adapt to students' individual ability levels.

Back to the Books

Although the online world has great test prep resources, you don't have to abandon actual test prep books. Many students find these books incredibly helpful in preparing for the SAT or ACT, and they're a great option for those who can't afford a prep course or don't have the time to commit to one. Whether you choose Barron's, Kaplan, or the Princeton Review, make sure that:

- ✔ You're comfortable with the book's style—after all, the review book will become your companion, so you'd better like the way it speaks to you.
- ✔ The book actually fits in your backpack.

Cope with Test Stress

You know deep down that your entire future will not be determined by a four-hour test (or a three-hour, forty-five-minute, twenty-two-second test, to be exact), but it's still difficult to calm your nerves when it comes to standardized exams—especially when you're walking into the classroom on test day. Let me provide you with some groundbreaking, scientifically researched, ingenious advice: *Do not be nervous.* Anxiety will only work against you.

Mary from Long Beach, New York, says that her first SAT score was lower than her practice test scores because she put so much pressure on herself to do well. "I was so nervous because I thought that everything was riding on this exam, and I totally froze," she explains. When she took the ACT in her senior year, Mary was much more relaxed and scored a 34 out of a possible 36. She attributes her stellar performance to the newfound ease that emerged once the stress of junior year was behind her.

But how can you alleviate junior-year stress when you're taking the exam in the middle of your junior year? You have no doubt been bombarded with well-meaning advice for months, all with the aim of reducing your anxiety on exam day. For instance, "Sit back, relax, and try some meditation. Picture yourself on a beautiful white beach with a crystal blue ocean and breathe deeply." Do you think that really works? (Yeah, neither do I.)

With so much advice being thrown at you, it's sometimes hard to determine exactly what you should do to calm your nerves and to optimize your performance on the SAT or ACT. For starters, Ed Carroll urges students not to deviate from their normal routine on test day. "Don't do anything that you've never done before. The morning of the SAT is not a good time to start drinking Red Bull," he says. He also cautions students against changing their prescriptions. There are lots of other tips that aren't earth-shaking but are nonetheless solid pieces of wisdom that can help give you a boost on exam day. This chart contrasts pre-exam advice that is glaringly obvious and the idiotic alternatives.

Standard Advice	Inferred Alternative
Get a good night's sleep the night before the test.	Stay up all night playing *Battleship*.
For an acute case of nerves, breathe deeply.	Hold your breath until your skin turns light blue.
Don't cram the day before.	Solve trigonometry problems for fifteen straight hours and stop a half hour before the exam.
Bring plenty of No. 2 pencils.	Bring a light wand and some glitter.
Bring an approved calculator.	Bring a black-market abacus.
Write down your social security number.	Write down your parole number.
Eat a good breakfast that morning.	Chow down on some beef burritos with a side of black beans the morning of the test.
Wear comfortable clothing to the test.	Wear assless chaps to the test.

Proctor Schmoctor

One of the most nerve-wracking parts on a standardized test, especially the SAT, is the information you fill in before the exam actually begins. How are you supposed to remember your social security number when you're so nervous you misspell your own name? And if you have a hyphenated last name, good luck keeping your heart rate under two hundred beats per minute.

Unfortunately, with very few exceptions, most proctors are not skilled at calming your nerves on exam day—particularly during the dreaded informational stage. Proctors are taught to stick to the script; they'll direct you to bubble in your name, address, social security number, and so on, while looking at you like a pit bull that's about to pounce. Many proctors *are* skilled, however, at heightening your anxiety by barking, "Start, stop, time's up!" and "Five minutes left. Wait, I mean fifteen. No, I mean five. Is there anyone here who can tell time?"

You have enough stress on exam day; don't let the proctor throw you. If you're stuck with a meanie, ignore the surly demeanor and nasty attitude when you ask a simple question, like "How long are our breaks?" or "What's the answer to question 16?" Take everything in stride and remind yourself that no one says they want to be an SAT proctor when they grow up.

There are a few things you can do to relieve some of the pressure (and create a much-needed diversion) on test day:

Grunt like a caveman every time you fill in "B."

Announce that the proctor is really an alien who was sent to Earth to bring back No. 2 pencils.

Tell your proctor that you have a phobia of bubbles and ask if there's an alternate way to submit your answers.

In the middle of the test, ask, "Does anyone else smell carbon monoxide?"

Take off your shirt and pants during the test and say you need to "air out."

SAT Subject Tests—The Hell Continues

As if the SAT and ACT weren't enough, the College Board decided to create SAT Subject Tests—because you need another reason to stay up until 4 a.m. There are twenty Subject Tests, running the gamut from math to physics to English to French, Italian, and many other languages (you're out of luck if you're fluent in Flemish though).

SAT Subject Tests (also known as the SAT IIs) are not a hard and fast requirement; some schools require three, some require two, and some don't require any. Doing well on these tests can only improve your application. As a former admissions officer at the University of Pennsylvania explains, "If you have a solid command over a certain subject area and are confident in your ability to do well on the SAT II, then you should take the test because this will only help your application."

The Subject Tests really exist for you to show off and underscore your strengths. For instance, if you excel at physics, you should definitely consider taking the Physics Subject Test. If you're an English egghead, stay away from the Math Level 2 exam. Stick to the subjects in which you feel most confident and experienced. Also, most test prep experts agree that you should take the test in the year you finish the course. So if you took biology as a sophomore, don't wait until junior year to take the Biology Subject Test. (Trust me: a year later you're not going to remember what a *megakaryocyte* is.) SAT II prep books and classes are available, but most likely the materials from your class will provide all the information you need.

If the prospect of taking the Subject Tests feels like the straw that could break your back, don't worry. On the standardized testing hierarchy of priority, these are near the bottom. As the head of a major New York City tutoring service says, "On the stress spectrum, the SAT IIs should come last. It's important to prepare and perform well, but chances are you've already prepared simply by taking the course in school."

Deep Thoughts on Standardized Tests

Some people are just not good test takers. I should know; I was one of them. I'll never reveal my SAT score (I'm taking that to the grave), but I can tell you that your academic record from your entire high school career is far more important than a four-hour exam you take during junior year. Your standardized test score will not wipe out four years of hard work.

Colleges know that not everyone excels at standardized tests. If your SAT or ACT score doesn't measure up to your academic performance, don't despair. Your score is not the sole determinant in college admissions; it is one factor among many, and it alone will not open or slam the door to any one school. With this in mind, avoid taking the SAT or ACT more than three times. After a while, you'll start to omit words from your sentences and expect other people to fill them in. This will become very annoying and you'll start losing friends.

CHAPTER 6

Surviving the College Tour: Please God, Not Another Library

"The clock tower was built in 1841, because before that nobody could agree on what time it was." Ah, the Gothic architecture, the perky tour guide, the useless facts you'll forget as soon as you get in the car for the ride home. There's nothing quite like the college tour.

No matter how many times you've taken the virtual tour online, perused the glossy brochures, or read your friends' blogs about the school, nothing can replace that gut feeling about a college that comes from seeing it in person. (Don't confuse this with the gut feeling that may come from eating in the cafeteria.) You can read Peterson's tome, *Four-Year Colleges*, all you want, but there is something about actually *being* on a campus that will give you a genuine sense of whether or not you can envision yourself in that environment for the next four years.

Aside from giving your parents a chance to humiliate you in front of a group of strangers, the purpose of the college tour is to acquaint you with the campus and let you absorb the school's atmosphere. Here are a few tips to remember on the tour:

- ✔ Be ready to smile and pretend you care about the number of books in the main library.

- ✔ Accept that you will be forced to see every single statue on campus. Try to summon the same enthusiasm as if you were seeing Michelangelo's *David*.

- ✔ Your tour guide will share some college traditions (most likely involving people running around naked) that will strike you as extremely stupid. Act as if you respect them.

- ✔ Don't ask too many questions about the "new research facility" being built. That's code for meth lab.

- ✔ Jot down what you like and don't like at each school. Otherwise, all of your impressions will merge and the only thing you'll remember is threatening to jump out of the car on the ride home.

Don't Judge a Campus by Its Urine

"My son dismissed a school as soon as we got out of the car," says Felicia, the mother of a college sophomore from Connecticut. "He took a look at the students and said, 'This isn't for me.'" That does seem a tad hasty. For many students, checking out a prospective college is similar to checking out a prospective date. Even though boils and excessive facial hair may be a turnoff (especially on girls), it's important to look deeper and not make any snap judgments. Your first impressions will likely be superficial and only part of a bigger, more complex picture.

"You should see the campus as thoroughly as you can," says Julie, a senior and tour guide at the University of Pennsylvania. "I notice that if a student doesn't immediately like the campus, he'll sort of tune out for the rest of the tour." But just like the girl with the goatee, any campus deserves more time to reveal its inner worth. Maybe you hate the architecture and quads, but that's just the surface. You have to do a lot more digging to really get to the heart of the school.

"I was going on a tour of Columbia with my family, and when we parked the car, the first thing we saw was a homeless guy peeing on the street," says Jonathan, a high school junior from Washington, DC. Fortunately, the man was a few blocks from the main part of campus, but still . . . No one wants to attend a college that also functions as a public toilet. "I was not ready to like Columbia after that first scene, but I got swept away by the people and the campus. We took the tour, and I ended up falling in love with the campus," Jonathan says. He did the smart thing: got past his first impression and instead focused on the tour and the school, which let him see it in a new light. He plans to apply to Columbia next year, early decision.

Amber, a freshman at the University of North Carolina at Chapel Hill, says she never dreamed of attending a big state school in the South. "I am a West Coast girl all the way." Originally, she set her sights on private schools in California and Oregon, but during spring break of her junior year in high school, she went to North Carolina with a friend who was interested in applying to UNC. Her friend asked her to go to the campus with her, and after taking the tour and walking around the campus, Amber was hooked. "The campus was amazing and the people were so friendly," she says. "I had this feeling that I would be really happy there."

Regardless of whether you're touring your dream school or one that your parents had to shove you in the trunk to see, approach the tour and campus with an open mind. If you can rid yourself of your negative first impressions and truly immerse yourself in the tour and explore what the school is about, you'll be much better equipped to decide whether you actually like it.

Before you embark on your college tour adventure, you will no doubt hear the same advice over and over again. This chart lists some common tips and the idiotic alternatives.

Obvious Advice	Inferred Alternative
Go while school is in session.	Go at three in the morning to check for vampires.
Check out the bulletin boards and the school newspaper.	Check out the literary magazine that three people read (two of whom are the editors).
Arrive at the tour early.	Arrive twenty minutes late and make the tour guide repeat everything you missed.
Ask questions about the school.	Ask questions about the existence of life on other planets.
Talk to current students.	Talk to the stray cats on campus.
Dress appropriately.	Tour the campus in a loincloth.

Establish Some Ground Rules with Your Parents

No college tour would be complete without one or both of your parents making you wonder, "Do I actually come from these people?" Fortunately, you can establish some ground rules to minimize inevitable embarrassment and leave the campus with your dignity intact. Sit down with Mom and Dad and urge them to:

✔ Refrain from dominating the discussion on the tour or in the information session. (If your parents make a bad impression, it won't reflect well on you.)

✔ Treat you as an adult. This means not using any cringe-inducing nicknames like "baby" or "pussycat" and asking questions like, "Would you like a snack from the breast or bottle?" You want to come across as independent and capable of making it through the night without a tuck-in from your mom.

✔ Keep quiet about your GPA, test scores, and awards in public, no matter how bright you are.

✔ Avoid asking other parents and students personal questions.

✔ Not say anything negative, even as a joke. Remarks like "Is the 'freshman fifteen' contagious?" won't endear you to an admissions committee.

✔ Phrase legitimate questions and concerns in the best way possible. (Refer them to this handy chart.)

Intelligent Questions Parents Can Ask	Questions That Make You Wish You Were Adopted
Does campus security provide vans to transport students at night?	Does campus security stun-gun students?
What services are offered at the student health center?	Is the health center equipped to deal with genital herpes?
How is the cafeteria food?	Is there a way to prevent my child from getting fat?
How is the career services center?	Can someone make sure my kid doesn't end up with a job at Costco?
Is financial aid available?	Will I have to sell one of my other children to pay the tuition?
What is the social scene like?	What are the chances of a member of the opposite sex touching my child?
What are some ways parents cope with having their child go away to college?	Would it be weird if I moved into my kid's dorm room?

Curb Their Enthusiasm: Make Mom and Dad Put Away Their Pom-Poms on the Tour

Tell your parents it's just embarrassing when they run to the bookstore to buy the logo-emblazoned hat, T-shirt, sweatshirt, keychain, and "Proud [school name] Parent" bumper sticker—because you haven't even been accepted yet. The same goes for shouting out school cheers when there's not some sort of game in session. "My mom thought it was cool to yell out 'Go Big Red!' when we passed a few people on the football team on the Cornell tour," says Hailey, a high school senior from Long Island, New York. "I was totally mortified. My mom was more into Cornell than I was, and I felt that everyone on the tour was like, 'Who's applying, you or your daughter?'"

Your parents should remember to keep their impressions to themselves. They may be dying for you to go to a specific school, but it's not going to help you if they break into the school anthem every ten minutes. Explain to Mom and Dad that although you appreciate their opinion, they need to stifle it during the tour and allow you to form your own impressions.

David from Connecticut recalls, "I was touring Yale with my parents and we got to this part where you're not supposed to step on this stone because if you do, the buildings might disintegrate. I thought it was really stupid, and I went out of my way to step on the stone. My parents started freaking out and explained to the tour guide that I was only joking and was completely serious about my desire to go to Yale. The tour guide didn't seem to care." David later pointed out to his parents that their reaction probably made a worse impression than his faux pas.

"A lot of parents think that their behavior on the tour is going to help get their kid in," says an admissions officer and former tour guide from a big private school in Washington, DC.

"I've never heard of parent enthusiasm tipping the scales in a student's favor." Unfortunately, it *can* work the other way. "A few years ago, a mother on one of our tours burst into the admissions office armed with trophies, certificates, and a copy of her child's IQ score," says a senior admissions officer from an elite private college in Massachusetts. "This did not reflect well upon her or her son. When this kind of thing happens, we are biased against the student, however unfair it is."

Help Mom and Dad Find the Middle Ground Between Giddiness and Apathy

There is also a danger when your parents show absolutely no interest in the school. Dawn from Ann Arbor, Michigan, went on a college tour in the Northeast with her parents. "I knew they didn't want me to leave the Midwest, but I thought they'd at least be somewhat supportive during the tours. My mom basically rolled her eyes the entire time, and my dad didn't stop checking his BlackBerry." Their behavior was so distracting that Dawn couldn't fully concentrate on getting to know the schools she was touring. "If it wasn't Northwestern or the University of Michigan, they weren't going to pay attention. I'm still applying to a few Northeast schools, but there's a part of me that wants to go back and do the tours again."

Ask your parents to be both supportive and interested— and help them to find the middle ground between joining the cheerleading squad and waiting in the parking lot during the entire tour. Reassure your parents that their opinion about a college matters to you, but also firmly remind them that ultimately, *your* opinion that is the one that counts. (Milk it while you can.)

After the College Tour and Info Session

So you took the tour and you're ready to go home. Not so fast—the tour is only one aspect of checking out a college. Once you've gotten the official spiel, you need to do a lot more legwork to solidify your impressions. Here are some strategies to help you dig a little deeper.

1. Talk to Students

Find current undergrads and ask them lots of questions. This is, hands down, the best thing you can do when visiting schools. Ask them about the classes, the social scene, the dorms, the food, the athletics—anything about any aspect of college life that crosses your mind. (Do not be surprised if people run away from you after question #47.)

2. Explore the Surrounding Area

Every now and then you may want to venture off campus and get to know the local turf. If the college is located in a city, check it out. Explore interesting cafés, bookshops, stores, parks, and any other spot that catches your eye. If you find yourself in a rural area, try milking some cows.

3. Stay Overnight

Many colleges offer a shadowing (overnight) program, so take advantage of these opportunities if possible. Staying with a student in the dorm is a great way to gain insight into the place where you could be living for the next four years. Remember that if you actually enroll, you will not be sleeping on the floor. Contact the school's admissions office for more information.

4. Observe a Few Classes

Unlike most high schools, there are many different types of classes in college, ranging from interactive seminars to massive lectures. Sitting in on a few courses can be a very enlightening experience and give you a sense of:

- ✔ The various class sizes—are the seminars small and discussion based or more like lectures?

- ✔ The level of student participation and interest—are students actively engaged or updating their Facebook profiles?

- ✔ Who is actually teaching the classes—professors or TAs (teaching assistants)?

Try to check out a class in a subject you may be interested in studying. Do not, however, speak up—nobody cares what freeloading visitors think. For details, contact the admissions office or the individual department.

5. Speak with Professors

After observing a class, approach the professor and ask how much time he or she spends with undergraduate students outside of class. Although no professor will say, "I ignore students because I don't give a rat's ass," you can get a feel for professors' availability by asking about office hours, the role of TAs, test and paper preparation and feedback, and so on.

6. Don't Overstay Your Welcome

Shadowing programs do not translate to "stalking programs." Don't be the annoying little high schooler who never leaves.

CHAPTER 7

When to Tell Your Parents It's Time to Start Seeing Other Children

"My mother thinks *she's* going to Williams," says Jared, a senior at an exclusive private high school in Manhattan. "She can tell you which vegetarian entrées they serve in the cafeteria on Thursdays." And Jared's not even a vegetarian. Jared is anxious to find out whether he'll be unpacking his bags in Williamstown next year. His mother, Ruth, is even more anxious. "I can't sleep anymore," Ruth confesses to me. "I keep thinking of things Jared should have included in his application." As worried as Jared is about his acceptance at Williams, he's even more worried about his mother. "I don't know how she'll take it if I don't get in," he says sadly.

You Want to Go *Where?*

From choosing which schools their kids should attend to actually writing the college essay, parents today are more involved in their children's college application process than ever before. Moms and dads of high school–aged children have gotten into the habit of viewing college acceptance as just another notch on one's proverbial status belt. Announcing to the world that Tommy's going to MIT is the equivalent of getting a new BMW— only Tommy is more likely to break down.

Sandra, from the suburbs of Philadelphia, Pennsylvania, was a straight-A student and a gifted actress and dancer. She nabbed the starring role in all of her school plays and was once told by a talent scout that she had a good shot at making it on Broadway. Her parents, however, insisted that she apply to Princeton. Although Sandra had the GPA and standardized test scores that met Princeton's criteria, she wanted to attend Bard, a small liberal arts school in the Hudson River Valley with a fantastic theater and dance program.

Sandra told her parents that she had absolutely no desire to go to Princeton. "It's like they didn't hear me," she says. "The more I told them how much I hated the idea, the harder they pushed me to apply." Sandra's parents didn't understand why their daughter wouldn't want to go to "one of the best schools in the country." They had attended public colleges and were adamant that their daughter receive the education they couldn't afford when they were her age. I asked Sandra's father, who is an attorney in Philadelphia, why he and his wife were so insistent on Princeton. "Do you know how many geniuses went to Princeton?" he asked me. "I mean, look at Einstein and John Nash." I was tempted to tell him that Cecil Terwilliger— Sideshow Bob's little brother on *The Simpsons*—was also an alum, but decided against it.

Sandra's parents refused to look at Bard with her. "They didn't understand why I would consider other schools when I had a shot at Princeton." Like many high schoolers, Sandra felt the pressure to attend a prestigious school. I didn't want to sway her one way or another, but thought she should know that Princeton's original name was the College of New Jersey and that it was located in Newark for nine years before moving to

Princeton in 1756. Loosely translated, the College of New Jersey means, "five miles from a toxic waste facility" in Aramaic. (Suddenly, *dei sub numine viget* doesn't sound so inspiring.)

When April rolled around, so did Sandra's acceptances to Princeton, Bard, and a host of other schools. Sandra had a decision to make: Should she make her parents happy or should she make herself happy? She decided to attend Bard. "My parents were devastated," she says. "My dad and I didn't talk for a month. He told my mom I was making the biggest mistake of my life."

If this scenario sounds familiar, it's imperative to tell your parents that *you* will be the one attending college for the next four years (or possibly longer, depending on your affinity for beer pong). It's a known fact that everyone has a constitutional right to "life, liberty, and deciding where to go to college without parental interference." It's never easy to confront your parents—especially about something as expensive as college. After all, since they may be shelling out around $50,000 a year in tuition, the least you can do is involve them in the college admissions process, allow them to obsess over every detail of the application, and let them choose your future school, right? Um . . . no. Although your parents are entitled to some input, where you apply and where you eventually go to school should be your decision. Be careful not to fall for the following parental arguments:

> We're paying for this, you little ingrate.
>
> We know what's best for you.
>
> When we were your age, we couldn't afford to go to college.
>
> It says on your birth certificate that your mother and I technically own you.
>
> We only conceived you because we wanted to brag about your going to Harvard.

If your parents aren't open to a particular college that you're very interested in, explain to them why you have your heart set on going there. They need to understand that there's logic behind your preferences and that you've thought this through carefully. Although at times it may seem that they want what's best for *them* rather than what's best for you, ultimately they want you to be happy.

Of course, you should consider your parents' feelings about college—approach the issue with the same open-mindedness that you expect from them. Mom and Dad may have legitimate reasons for wanting you to attend (or not attend) a certain school. I know iPods were specifically designed for tuning out parents, but there's a chance that they may be making valid points, so hear them out. In some cases, parents are capable of saying something that makes sense or pointing out something that you may have overlooked. If this happens, remind yourself that since humans have landed on the moon, anything's possible.

What to Do When Communication Is Failing

Talking to your mom and dad is easier said than done, right? Dr. Jonathan Tobkes, a child and adolescent psychiatrist based in New York City, says, "The nature of the parent-teenager relationship is characterized by a fundamental disconnect." In other words, sometimes you don't get your parents and they don't get you. Dr. Tobkes has some suggestions for breaking through the impasse.

Seek a Third Party to Help Resolve the Dispute

When you feel that you're just not getting through to Mom and Dad, Dr. Tobkes suggests bringing in a third party. Try not to involve someone you or your parents know well; your weird Aunt Penelope may be biased. School psychologists or social workers can be very helpful in resolving a conflict, provided that they can serve as impartial observers. To set up a meeting, get in touch with your school psychologist. Family therapy can also be a good solution, particularly if other methods haven't been successful.

Whether you seek out a school psychologist, social worker, or family therapist, Dr. Tobkes suggests that you and your parents try an exercise called "reflection." This technique has two purposes: to allow you to openly express your feelings and to facilitate understanding of the other party's point of view. After one person speaks, the other must repeat what was said, verbatim. For example, if a father and daughter were engaging in reflection, the father may say, "I'm controlling how you do your application because I don't want you to make a mistake." The daughter must repeat the line, word for word. "This exercise helps to get the other person's perspective," says Dr. Tobkes. "The third party is essentially neutral and is only there to facilitate discussion." The point of reflection is to find a middle ground where both parties are content. If the father feels compelled to control the application process, maybe he can agree to back down and let his daughter take charge, but still have an influence; perhaps she can discuss her ideas for the essay with him or let him review the final application.

Get to the Root of the Problem

It's important for you and your parents to resolve the conflicts that emerge about college sooner rather than later, because they could resurface later in life if they aren't addressed. "Usually, arguments about the college process are symptomatic of something larger," Dr. Tobkes says. Maybe your father needs to feel in control at all times, and that's why he's so gung-ho about examining every aspect of your application. Maybe your mother has lived vicariously through your achievements for the past eighteen years, and that's why she thinks she's the one getting into college when the acceptance letter arrives.

Take a step back and see whether there's a pattern. Has your dad always tried to control how you do things? Does your mom experience your successes and failures as her own? If you can identify a pattern, the conflict between you and your parents about college is most likely a manifestation of that pattern. Nip it in the bud before it gets out of hand—it's better to air your grievances *now* than be in family therapy for the next thirty years. Once you've identified a recurring tendency, alert your parents and work together to try to break the cycle and alter any unhealthy behavior. Otherwise, this problem could materialize again and again in the future. Do you really want your dad to tell you what to have for breakfast when you're forty? Or your mom to call your mortgage broker and cry hysterically because you weren't granted a loan?

Learn Your Parents' First Names

Try doing some activities together that you'll both enjoy—just make sure that activity isn't filling out the Common Application. Spending time together is a great way to connect with your parents and take a break from the stressful application process. You might be surprised to learn that your parents are capable of starting a conversation without saying, "How are those applications going, sport?"

Understand Why Your Parents Are Scared

Remember when your parents first brought you home from the hospital? Of course you don't—you were most likely three days old! But your parents do, and it was probably the happiest (or most overrated) moment of their lives. For the past eighteen years or so, your parents have worked very hard to protect you. They know that come September, there's nothing to stop you from eating whipped cream and s'mores for dinner. In fact, that's just one of many reasons why your parents may wake up in the middle of the night with the sheets soaked. It's not that they weren't potty-trained—it's that the prospect of you operating as an independent adult is terrifying.

As if the idea of you going to class in the winter without zipping up your Gore-Tex jacket isn't frightening enough, your parents are coming to grips with the fact that they have no control over where you'll be accepted to college. "Essentially, your parents are abdicating control of your destiny to a bunch of strangers," says Ronnie Einhorn, Ph.D., a school psychologist at New Rochelle High School in New Rochelle, New York. "To many parents, it's these faceless admissions officers who have all the power." Dr. Einhorn says that because most parents see their children as extensions of themselves, they perceive their children's successes and failures as direct reflections not only of their parenting skills but also of who they are. It is this psychology that propels bumper stickers like "My Child Is an Honors Student" as opposed to ones like "My Kid Is a Loser We Keep in the Basement."

Your parents mean well, but their fear and worry may cause them to step over the line from time to time. Be aware that parental anxiety can manifest itself in many different ways: from excessive pressure to get into a good school to overinvolvement in your application to even downright nastiness. Unfortunately, *you* are probably the primary outlet for channeling all that nervous energy. Nevertheless, try to appreciate where you parents are coming from. The next time your mother screams at you for procrastinating on your college essay, remember that she's acting from a primal need to cushion you from the harsh vicissitudes of college admissions and a deep-seated fear of your impending adulthood. Or something like that.

Typical Exchanges Between Parent and Child

To help you cope with your frustration, the following are a few documented examples of healthy versus anxiety-fueled exchanges between the college-bound student and the parent. They should help you gauge where your parents fall on the college support spectrum.

Mom: How are those college applications going?
Johnny: Fine.
Mom: Great! Let me know if you need me to look anything over.

Mom: How are those college applications going?
Johnny: Fine.
Mom: Great—just remember that if you don't get into a top-twenty school, you're dead to me.

Jane: Dad, I'm trying to answer a short-essay question How would you describe me in twenty-five words or less?
Dad: Perfect.
Dad and Jane hug.

Jane: Dad, I'm trying to answer a short-essay question. How would you describe me in twenty-five words or less?
Dad: Disappointing.
Jane runs to her room.

Jimmy: I think I want to go to an art school.
Mom: That's a wonderful idea! You're so talented.
Jimmy: I love you, Mom.

Jimmy: I think I want to go to an art school.
Mom: Remember that clay vase you made for me? I thought it was a toilet.
Jimmy starts to cry.

How to Deal with Overbearing Parents

You can't take it anymore. Your dad has embarrassed you on too many college tours to count, and your mom asked an admissions officer if being "the cutest munchkin in the senior class" will help you get in. "My parents actually sent my Common Application without telling me," says Lisa from Middletown, New Jersey. "They told me they looked it over and decided it was done." Ashley from Millbrae, California, had a similar experience, although she intercepted her application before it made it into the mail. "My dad hijacked my college essay, even though I wanted to be an English major," she says. "He wrote about whale mating rituals and somehow compared that to my desire to go to this particular school. It was totally inappropriate—not to mention like a thousand words over the limit."

If your parents do one or all of the following—forge your signature, write your essay, arrange college tours without your permission, dominate the discussion at information sessions, or dress up as an admissions officer for Halloween—then you have two options:

1. Run away from home
2. Make a few suggestions

Tell your parents that while you appreciate their support, their obsessive-compulsive, control-freakish behavior is becoming a tad annoying. Ask Mom and Dad to read the following section, memorize it, and repeat it verbatim three times a day. If they don't go for that, tell them you'll be satisfied if they mull it over for a day or two.

✔ Let your child apply where she wants, even if it's not the school of your dreams.

✔ If paying for school is an issue, have a candid talk about it. Explain that attending certain schools may not be possible because of prohibitive costs.

✔ If you have real reservations about your child's choice of school, sit down with him and explain why you're concerned. If your fears are unfounded, admit that your judgment was premature. (If you can't bring yourself to verbalize that, giving him a new car says the same thing.)

✔ Remember that your child may not want the same things that you do. She has different tastes, preferences, and interests. Respect her ability to make an independent choice.

✔ Don't buy a college sticker for the car until your child has been accepted.

✔ Don't get caught up in where your neighbor's kid is applying—this has nothing to do with your child. Keep the competition limited to who has the better barbecue grill and perkiest vegetable garden.

✔ If your involvement with your child's applications becomes obsessive, talk to other parents who have gone through the experience and ask them how they coped with it. Either that, or think about taking up online poker.

✔ Don't ever say, "I know more about this than you do"—no matter how tempted you are.

✔ Remain supportive, but don't cross the line between support and interference. For example, "Do you need help proofreading your essay?" is preferable to "This garbage needs to be rewritten."

✔ Bear in mind that the happiest parents are the ones whose child is going to the school where *he* thinks he'll be happiest.

✔ Realize that your child's worth (and your success as a parent) is not measured by the thickness of the envelope that comes in December or April.

✔ Start planting the seeds now for controlling grad school.

If your parents don't heed any of this advice—or deny that their interest in your college application is even remotely overzealous—have them take the following quiz. Be prepared to hear, "What, me overbearing?"

Quiz: Are You an Overbearing Parent?

1. Your kid tells you she got a B– on an American History exam. You:

   A) Scream, "How can you ruin your life like that?" as loudly as possible.

   B) Tell her that you're satisfied as long as she did her best.

   C) Suggest reenacting the Revolutionary War together instead of going to homecoming.

   D) Casually mention the three ancillary causes of the Boston Tea party in every conversation.

2. You're driving your son to his college interview. You:

   A) Go to the interview with him—after all, you can do a much better job of conveying who he is than he can.

   B) Drop him off and wish him good luck.

   C) Climb up on the roof, squeeze down the chimney, and park yourself one table over to overhear the entire thing.

   D) Wire-tap him in case you need to feed him answers.

3. Your kid is taking the SAT in a few months. You:

    A) Repaper her room in vocabulary flashcards.

    B) Ask what you can do to help her prepare.

    C) Talk about how "hip" quadratic equation tattoos are.

    D) Dip into her 529 savings plan to pay for private tutors.

4. You see your child's essay on the kitchen table. You:

    A) Take a cursory read and make a few changes.

    B) Don't look at it yet—you wouldn't feel comfortable without permission.

    C) Change the title from "Why I Admire Mother Teresa" to "Why I'm Just Like Mother Teresa."

    D) Work the phrase "gift to mankind" into every other sentence.

5. You're at an information session at your kid's dream school. You:

    A) Ask if the school has a special cafeteria where the geniuses eat.

    B) Resist the urge to speak, and encourage your child to ask questions.

    C) Demand to know what percentage of students lose their virginity by sophomore year.

    D) Ask to sit in on an admissions meeting "to get a better idea of the school's criteria."

If you answered "B" to all of the above questions, then you fall into the 0.00076 percent of parents who are supportive, kind, and understanding. If you answered anything other than "B," then you should never have become a parent in the first place. Just kidding! You are actually a normal, concerned parent—you've simply gotten a little too swept up in the frenzy of the college admissions process. Take a look at those B answers again, and see whether emulating them wouldn't make the process more sane for both you and your child.

Don't Let College Applications Come Between You and Your Parents

You need to accept certain things in life: no one looks sexy in a marching band uniform, Mounds is a very underrated candy bar, and you will fight with your parents about college. In fact, if you don't get into arguments with them about this topic, I suggest reexamining your relationship.

The best way to talk to your parents is—to talk to your parents. Your mom and dad can't guess what you're thinking; it's your job to tell them directly. The main complaint I hear from students is that their parents don't listen to them. If your parents are tuning you out, try to arrange some alone time with them. Whether it's going out to dinner, taking a drive, or bungee jumping, take this opportunity to convey how you feel in a low-pressure, relaxed environment.

A private college counselor told me about a student who loved playing basketball. Her mother, however, thought it would look much better to colleges if her daughter volunteered at a hospital instead. When the counselor asked the student why she quit basketball, she replied, "Because my mom made me." The counselor decided to have a talk with the girl's mother. "I told her to ask her daughter if she was happy about dropping basketball." When the mother did that, her daughter told her how much she missed playing the sport. The next day, with her mom's approval, she rejoined the basketball team.

Sometimes all it takes is simple communication. Respect your parents' input, but be honest with them, and don't be afraid to stand up for yourself. If all else fails, see which of the following techniques will distract your parents and make your future the last subject they want to talk about.

Ten Ways to Get Your Parents to Back Off the Whole College Thing

1. Announce that instead of going to college, you're going to join the circus as a sad clown.

2. Inform them that high school graduates are the highest-paid employees on the paper route.

3. Right before your parents go to bed, ask them if they've drawn up a will, and laugh in a particularly creepy way.

4. Wear a T-shirt that says "College taught me about thongs and bongs" to Thanksgiving dinner.

5. Call the alumni office of your parents' first-choice school and ask to contact their least successful graduate.

6. Inform your parents that "college dormitory" is another name for "breeding ground of STDs."

7. Threaten to attend an all-girls' school (if you're a boy).

8. Remind them that you don't need a college degree to slice pastrami.

9. Express how excited you are to major in Transgender Studies.

10. Look them in the eye and ask if spending over $200,000 on you is worth it.

CHAPTER 8

The Art of Asking and/or Threatening Teachers for a Good Recommendation

There are a few cases in which you should definitely not ask a teacher to write you a recommendation letter for college:

> The teacher still doesn't know your name.
>
> The teacher has suggested that you be held back.
>
> On Parents' Night, the teacher asked your parents if they had ever considered giving you up for adoption.
>
> The teacher has never heard you speak.

Many students make the mistake of assuming that college admissions officers barely glance at the recommendation letters from teachers. But they're wrong. Admissions officers take these letters very seriously. If the letters are not supportive or do not seem consistent with the student's application, the file edges closer to the "Reject" pile.

It's vital to approach the right teachers for your letters—only those who you are absolutely, positively, indubitably, unquestionably sure will write you a very strong letter. If you are not sure of this, don't even ask. Teachers know that part of their job is to write recommendations for college. If they like you, in most cases they'll gladly write you a supportive letter. If they don't like you, the letter will most likely not be glowing and could considerably weaken your application.

"I suggest that students pick a teacher they've really connected with," says Bob Sweeney, a guidance counselor at Mamaroneck High School in Mamaroneck, New York. Many guidance counselors and admission officers concur that it doesn't necessarily have to be a teacher from your junior or senior year. The quality of your relationship with your teacher is far more important than the year in which you took his or her class.

An admissions officer at a private university in upstate New York told me that one of the most moving recommendations she ever read was from a teacher who had nearly failed the student out of AP Physics. "The teacher was so impressed by how hard the student tried to grasp the material. Learning how the kid dealt with struggling in the class gave us a lot of insight into the character of that person," she says. As a general rule it's not a good idea to submit a letter from a teacher who might fail you. But even if you don't ace a class, a pattern of consistent effort and participation will most likely be enough incentive for a teacher to write a positive letter.

How to Approach Your Teacher

There are effective ways and not-so-effective ways to request a recommendation from your teacher. Refer to the chart on the next page for a few options.

Right Way to Ask Your Teacher	Wrong Way to Ask Your Teacher
I know you're busy, but would you consider writing my college recommendation letter?	I'm guessing you don't have a lot going on in your personal life, so can you write my letter?
I really enjoy your class and would be honored if you wrote me a recommendation letter for college.	Your class sucked, but you can repay me by writing this letter.
Could I talk to you after class about possibly writing me a recommendation?	It's not like teaching is a real job, so you need some way to justify your existence. How about writing my college rec?
I've always admired you and hope you can write my recommendation; it would mean a lot to me.	I didn't mean it when I said you look like a demented chimpanzee on Ratemyteacher.com. Please write this.
I would love for you to write my recommendation letter, but I understand if you can't.	My parents pay your salary, so it's not like you can say no.
Would you think about writing my recommendation letter? I feel like you've gotten to know me well.	You're Plan B in case the custodian says no.

What Teachers Are Supposed to Convey in the Letter

When it comes to the recommendation letter, your teacher is supposed to be like your grandmother—he or she has carte blanche to brag about you until it makes other people sick. But in this case, those "other people" form an admissions committee who depend on these letters as outside validation that you're not a psycho. There are four key components your teacher should write about.

✔ Your intellectual gifts (if you don't have any, he or she should make something up)

✔ Your participation (interactions and involvement in the class)

✔ Your character (how you conduct yourself and treat your peers)

✔ Your extracurriculars (outside pursuits, talents, and activities)

Your Intellectual Gifts

First and foremost, the teacher recommendation should stress your smarts, which you've exhibited by your excellent academic performance. Admissions officers get excited when they learn the applicant has a thirst for knowledge; it makes them believe you will be an active intellectual member of the college community. (Keep it to yourself that you plan on using the next four years to catch up on your sleep.)

Your Participation

Admissions committees want to get a sense of your academic talents as seen through the eyes of an educator. They are also looking for a glimpse of your interactions and level of participation in the classroom. Do you ask insightful questions? Are you a leader in group projects? Do you doodle pictures of nuclear weapons during class discussions?

When admissions officers are asked what they look for in recommendation letters, they love to throw around phrases like "intellectual vitality" and "intellectual curiosity." Basically, they want to know whether you've asked questions in class other than "Can I take a leak?" Your recommendation letters inform admissions officers what kind of student you are.

There are four basic categories of students:

1. **The shy, quiet student.** This student does not say anything in class for the entire academic year. He most likely comes home from school, has milk and chocolate-chip cookies, and proceeds to torture animals.

2. **The student who interjects once in a while.** This student is like the shy, quiet type but knows she must say something every now and then or else people will assume she is mute.

3. **The student who regularly participates.** Not too quiet and not too loud, this student is a rare breed and highly coveted by teachers. Yes, he also eats porridge that is not too hot and not too cold, and is occasionally called "Goldilocks."

4. **The annoying student who constantly has her hand up.** This student truly believes everything that comes out of her mouth is extremely important and of interest to everybody. Clearly, the student's favorite sound is her own voice, which often stimulates the gag reflex in anyone around her.

Try to aim for classification as type #3 if you want a stellar recommendation. Falling into one of three other types will not likely inspire your teacher to write a rave review, unless she's recommending you for inpatient treatment or a correctional facility. A good rule of thumb is to participate in class only when you have something meaningful to contribute. Don't ask questions and make comments simply for the sake of taking up air. You can do that once you're a philosophy major in college.

Your Character

There's no need for your teacher to know that you kick puppies to blow off steam. As long as your teacher thinks you are a kind, decent, law-abiding human being, he or she will be able to attest to your upstanding character. Lay the groundwork; approaching your teacher to write your recommendation should not be the first display of politeness that she's seen from you; you should have a strong track record of mature behavior in class. Your teacher is aware of how you handle yourself in the classroom and how you interact with others. As long as you've always been respectful and courteous and haven't physically attacked anyone, you should get a thumbs-up in the character department.

Your Extracurriculars

Let your teacher know what you're up to outside of school. You want him or her to talk up your extracurricular pursuits in the recommendation later, as this will lend credence to your supposed well-roundedness. Do whatever you can to make your teacher aware that you are a productive and interesting person outside the classroom. For instance, you can casually say, "Sometimes I like to take baths with my Cabbage Patch Kids. Did you know I have the world's largest collection?" or "You have a great smile—it reminds me of a battered woman I volunteer with every Tuesday and Thursday from 4:00 to 5:30," or "Would you like to meet me for a friendly duel after school so I can practice my fencing?"

The best—and most efficient—way of cluing your teacher into your outside pursuits is (though I hate to use the dreaded phrase) submitting a "brag sheet." Type up a comprehensive list of your interests, hobbies, participation in sports and clubs, and other outside pursuits and hand it to your teacher after she's agreed to write your letter. Do not expect your teacher to prostrate herself before you.

Typical Brag Sheet

Activities and Interests to Include

✔ Vice president of the senior class

✔ Plays oboe in the school orchestra

✔ Works at Baskin-Robbins after school

✔ Member of the cross-country team

Things to Leave Off the Brag Sheet

✘ Founder of the local squirrel-worshipping cult

✘ Creates art installations from toenail clippings

✘ Anti-ageism activist: forces old ladies to stand up on the bus

✘ Child safety advocate: makes bomb threats at nursery schools to check evacuation procedures

Sample Recommendation Letters

The following letters are representative examples of three basic categories of teacher recommendations. If your teachers are likely to write anything similar to these samples, hopefully the other elements of your application will compensate.

Category 1:
"I'm Writing This Because Child Services Is Forcing Me"

To Whom It May Concern:

It is my pleasure to support Jake Cunningham's candidacy for the class of 20__. I have had the pleasure of being Jake's math teacher for the past year.

Jake is a leader. He has led some of the most exciting gang fights in our school's history. He has been an agent of innovation and reform, leading the school to install various exciting upgrades, like metal detectors and security guards. All I have to say is: don't cut in front of this guy in the cafeteria.

Jake is an active and passionate participant in class discussions. He has thrown his desk through the window to make a point, and he once set a substitute teacher's hair on fire when she mispronounced his name.

Jake is very intellectually curious; when he wants a question answered, he will go to great lengths to satisfy his knowledge, such as showing up at my kids' preschool. Jake has a kind of persistence and ingenuity that is unusual in a student, coupled with a remarkable generosity. He was relentless in asking me for a recommendation; once I agreed, he offered to replace all of the tires he had slashed on my car.

Jake's gifts, talents, and pocket knife will ensure that he leaves an indelible mark on any college he attends.

Godspeed,

Harry Winthrop
Algebra Teacher

P.S. I've enclosed a recent picture of Jake for you to forward to campus security.

Category 2:
"I'm in Love with This Student Because She Puts the Brown in Brownnose"

To Whom It May Concern:

Mary is the most outstanding individual who has ever been born. If I were to name the next president of the United States, it would be Mary Whittington.

Mary has taken my World History, AP History, and Economics classes. Mary even wrote to the school board and obtained special permission to sit on my desk during class instead of at a regular desk like the other (less motivated) students.

Mary always asks extremely insightful questions, such as, "Miss Sterling, do many people mistake you for a Brazilian supermodel?" and "What did you think of the Double Chocolate Devil's Food Delight cake I baked for the teachers' lounge?" Mary also displays incredible initiative. For the past few months, she has been writing to Harvard University requesting that they grant me an honorary Ph.D. (Note that I've never been to Cambridge, Massachusetts, in my entire life.)

The phrase "academically gifted" doesn't even begin to describe Mary. She records all of my lectures, impeccably transcribes them, then demonstrates her critical thinking by rephrasing exactly what I've said on all of her exams and papers. Reading anything Mary writes is a pleasure.

Mary is a classroom leader. She has no tolerance for other students wasting time by sharing their opinions, and she takes it upon herself to interject and tell them to stop babbling. This saves me a lot of headaches.

Mary's zeal for learning, her drive to get to the intellectual heart of complex issues, and her passionate commitment to washing my car every Friday make her a standout student. I will be very sorry to see her go.

Best,

Susan D. Sterling
SDS/mw

Category 3:
"I Don't Know Who This Student Is, But What the Hell, I'll Write It"

To Whom It May Concern:

I fully support student X's candidacy to your university. Student X and I have grown close over the years. I once saw him accidentally go into the faculty men's restroom and told him to get out. I think that was two years ago, but it seems like yesterday. Then last year I saw him pull out of his parking space.

Student X is definitely a living, breathing person with a pulse. He doesn't look like he would murder anyone, his hair isn't that greasy, and from what I can see he has an enviable blue Jansport backpack.

Student X will surely be a terrific asset to your school. (Let me know what that is when he gets there.)

Sincerely,

Steve Baum
Biology Teacher

The Elements of an Effective Teacher Recommendation

It's your teacher's job to paint a compelling picture of you as an individual beyond your GPA and test scores. He should give concrete examples that illustrate who you are as a person. The more specific the examples, the better. For instance, "Hector is a leader" is not as effective as, "Hector bites others if they don't listen to what he says." Anecdotes are also great. Stories are more powerful and memorable than a list of dry adjectives. If possible, your teacher should aim to make the letter somewhat entertaining and interesting to read. Try to choose a teacher with a little personality—if he doesn't have one, chances are he won't be able to capture yours.

Refrain from Asking to See— or Rewrite—the Letter

It's a good idea to waive your right to see your teacher recommendation. Colleges want to be sure you had no direct influence over the content of the letter. If you still care about the letter after your acceptance, you can ask your teacher to share it then—but don't be surprised if she's already burned it.

Writing the Essay: The Line Between Good and Bad Is Thinner Than You Think

Before you begin writing your essay, you need to choose an interesting, meaningful subject. Most of the essay prompts on college applications are fairly open-ended, so it's really up to you to come up with a compelling topic. The following are examples of good versus good-for-nothing essay subjects.

Good Topics	Bad Topics
My Intel science project explores the origins of an itch.	Why I enjoy scratching myself.
Why my dog is my best friend.	Why my dog is my only friend.
Why my grandmother had a profound influence on my life.	My grandma died and left me a boatload of money.
The homeless need better security.	I steal booze from the homeless.
My trip to India taught me about resilience and the power of hope.	In India, the cows crap right in the street.

So how do you approach the essay? Should you just dive right in, like with a typical homework assignment? Not quite—writing an outstanding college essay requires some careful reflection, research, and strategizing. The following tips will help give you the preparation and confidence you need to ace the essay:

✔ Start reading books at least a few months before you begin your essay. By books, I don't mean *Where the Wild Things Are.* Read the classics: Tolstoy, Austen, Dickens, Chekhov, Dostoevsky, Flaubert, Bulgakov—anything by a dead white guy is a good bet. Quality reading leads to quality writing. You'll be surprised at how much your vocabulary and thought processes improve by reading books written by authors with unpronounceable names.

✔ Keep a daily diary. You don't have to write about your innermost thoughts and feelings—you're not writing a Lifetime special. You can write about *any-thing*: your activities, your friends, your family, your fears, your hopes, your plan for world domination, and so on. The mere act of doing this every day will exercise your writing muscles and give you the confidence to tackle the essay.

✔ Ask a friend to write a short essay about you. What's the most interesting thing you've ever done? What makes you a unique person? If the answer to the second question is "a third nipple," then you may want to go with the first one. This will let you see yourself from another's perspective and may shed some light on how you affect the people you care about.

✔ Think about how you would describe yourself to a stranger. If you had only three minutes to communicate your "essence," what would you tell that person? (Don't try this out on someone sitting in an adjacent restroom stall.)

✔ Become conscious of the activities, routines, or rituals that are meaningful to you: Maybe it's taking out the garbage, maybe it's feeding your dog, maybe it's biking to school, maybe it's your weekly bonding sessions with your parole officer. These seemingly little things often make great essay subjects. The routine itself doesn't have to be earth-shattering—it's the reason *why* it's special to you that matters.

✔ Do not, under any circumstances, plagiarize. I know the Romans got away with doing it to the Greeks, but the academic world has very strict standards when it comes to intellectual property. So unless you're revamping an entire legacy of cultural myths, don't go there.

✔ Do not read too many sample essays. Stay away from anthologies or websites with names like *100 Best College Essays*. You want your essay to be solely your product, so try to avoid situations in which other people's ideas could seep in. There's no harm in checking out a few sample essays, but don't go overboard.

✔ Seek your teachers' input. Teachers are often underutilized resources. Your English teacher is familiar with the English language—ask him or her to review your essay. If you'd like further feedback, ask another teacher to review it. (Your gym teacher would probably love a break from dodgeball.)

✔ Make sure your parents are the last people to see your essay, if possible. They may be tempted to interfere too much and could drastically change your voice, so show them the essay when it's almost finished. It's fine to incorporate any helpful feedback, but the voice should still be *yours*.

Keep Your Parents Away from the Essay (Until It's Mostly Done)

Mom and Dad may give you the following reasons why you must let them help you tackle the college essay:

They know you better than anyone else (including yourself).

They think you're incapable of writing basic English.

They believe their input is so invaluable you'll never get in anywhere without it.

They'll cut off your food supply if you say no.

Although it may be tempting to ask your parents for help with the essay, resist the urge. Because your parents are too close to you and the admissions process, their input will probably not be as helpful as they think. Your best strategy is to wait until the essay is in a solid (almost) final state and has been viewed by other, more objective people (teachers, friends, or other less biased sources). "We've seen so many essays where it's evident that a parent, aunt, best friend, or teacher made multiple revisions and the student didn't seem very focused," says an admissions officer from an Ivy League school. If your parents interfere too much with your essay, chances are it won't accurately reflect you.

It's important to follow your instincts when it comes to the essay. Jennifer, a high school senior from New Jersey, says that she was very happy with her essay when she asked her mom for input. She was applying to Cornell and had written about how her personal experiences led to her career goal of becoming a doctor. "My mom thought it would be better to change the entire format and make the essay a dialogue between me and a future patient," Jennifer says. "I'm very close with my mom and trust her, so I did change the essay. The problem was, it seemed totally forced." Jennifer showed her revised essay to her English teacher, who suggested she go back to the original format. "It was a huge relief," Jennifer says. "I know my mom was trying to help, but the essay didn't feel right with her suggestions."

Although you need to follow your gut feeling when it comes to the essay, don't completely ignore your parents' input. Donovan from Orlando, Florida, asked his father what he thought of his finished essay. His dad's response: "As I read it I began to think about all the laundry I had to do. There was no spark." That reaction "scared the hell out of me," Donovan admits. "I was writing about a cause I was passionate about—universal health care—and I asked my dad how to add more 'oomph' to my writing." Donovan's father suggested that he write about his personal experiences with the uninsured patients he encountered while working at a medical office. His essay turned from a dry treatise into a thoughtful, insightful piece that revealed a lot about him. "I really thank my dad for helping me. He made me realize I could do so much more with my essay."

When it comes to your parents and your essay, remember the following hints:

Your parents mean well, but take their criticism with a grain of salt.

Decline any offers from your parents to write your essay for you.

Do not entitle your essay "I'm Going to College So I No Longer Have to See My Parents on a Daily Basis."

What Admissions Officers Really Think of Your Essay

Okay, so it's hell to write an admissions essay. But guess what? It's also hell to read one—and admissions officers read thousands every year. The many admissions officers I spoke with confirmed that, yes, the essay *does* make a difference in your application. However, the extent of that difference varies based on your academic record, the college's admissions philosophy, and how boring your essay is. Based on my interviews with admissions officers from around the country, students' essays seem to fall into seven main categories.

1. The Attempt-at-Humor Essay

An admissions officer from an Ivy League school recalls an essay entitled "Why Women Should No Longer Be Able to Vote." It was supposed to be a satire, but the admissions officer didn't know exactly what the essay was satirizing. "I didn't realize until the end that the student actually supported women's rights," she says. "It came off as weird, and by the end I was not a big fan of the applicant." You can definitely add some mild humor, but don't test your funny bone in the admissions essay and push the envelope. Save it for open mike night.

2. The Cry-for-Help Essay

The essay is not the place to talk about your psychological issues. An admissions officer from a small liberal arts school in Minnesota told me that one applicant wrote about how she felt like Gregor in Kafka's *Metamorphosis*: she described how everyone around her made her feel trapped and suffocated and how much she was looking forward to being set free in college. Needless to say, the admissions officer was worried about the emotional well-being of the applicant. If you're teeming with angst, suffering, and emotional strife, don't make the essay your outlet. If you do, the college might send you a referral to a shrink instead of an acceptance letter.

3. The I-Make-the-World-a-Better-Place Essay

The following are the actual opening sentences of a student's essay about volunteering at a nursing home: "They're old, with sagging skin and sunken eyes, deflated souls and burnt breath, playing bingo in the game room. But I could see a faint glimmer of hope flash in their eyes when I walked in the room. They saw me and knew that at that very moment, life got a lot better." (The applicant neglected to mention that the same thing happened five minutes later when a hyper golden retriever entered the room.) Unless you're the messiah, do not tell the admissions committee that you were put on earth to save the world.

4. The Laying-It-on-Too-Thick Essay

There are good and bad ways to let a school know how much you want in. A good way is to write about how interested you are in attending the college and how you envision yourself as part of the community. A bad way is to write about being on your deathbed seventy years from now, as one student did. The applicant, who applied to a big state school, talked about how his life was complete because he had attended that particular university. In the essay, he tells his friends and relatives how significant and life-changing his college experience was. A sappy, sentimental approach works at weddings and funerals, but not in the college essay.

5. The Way-Too-Broad-a-Topic Essay

Admissions officers can immediately tell when a student is trying to wow them with a broad, philosophical, life-altering topic. More often than not, this will rub an admissions officer the wrong way. You can't answer the meaning of life in your essay, so don't even try. Do not pontificate over such vast issues such as death, religion, war, or the nature of Bert and Ernie's relationship. The "smaller" the topic, the more digestible the essay.

6. The I've-Overcome-So-Many-Obstacles Essay

One student wrote her college essay about failing her road test seven times. Bad parallel parking is not the kind of obstacle that's going to move an admissions officer. Superficial obstacles like fighting with a friend or getting grounded for a month are not worthy of an essay. If you want to pursue this topic, think about challenges that you have truly worked hard to overcome, like doing well in a difficult class, adjusting to a new town and high school, or persevering with a sport. Admissions officers want to see how you grew from overcoming real challenges.

7. The My-Personal-Growth-Will-Make-You-Sick Essay

An admissions officer at a medium-sized private school in Ohio recalls an applicant who wrote about how he was consistently late for school and had a habit of mindlessly stepping on the flowers in the school's yard as a shortcut to class. One day a janitor yelled at him and told him that he had worked hard to grow the flowers. This scolding prompted a convenient epiphany from the applicant: He realized that all of life is precious, all things delicate, and that he would enjoy life more if he "took time to smell the roses." Would you let this guy into your college?

Write a Strong Essay That Reflects You

The more you focus on what you think admissions officers want to hear, the more contrived and insincere your essay will be. It may sound strange, but the harder you try with the essay, the worse it will become. You want your essay to be clear, consistent, and strong, but don't overreach in either the topic or the writing. It's not necessary to write fifteen drafts or tinker with it endlessly—if you do, it will probably sound forced. Allow the essay to retain a spark of freshness. You don't even have to be a great writer to write a great essay. You just have to be sincere. Sincerity and earnestness go a lot further than artificial grandiosity.

Don't Forget to Answer the Question

You'd be surprised how many people don't actually address the essay question they are "answering." Regardless of how irrelevant the question seems, it is imperative that you construct your essay around answering it. Do not be tangential. If you're responding to "Why are you a good fit for this college?" don't talk about how much you love your grandmother. Your essay must be lean and mean and to the point. Every sentence, thought, and idea must be related to the question: irrelevance will not score you any points.

Do not waste time marveling at the ridiculousness of an essay question. For now, all you can do is humor the admissions committee by responding as if it's the deepest, most fascinating query you've ever seen. If you become an admissions officer one day, you can fight to change the system and replace the standard essay questions with the following, which would make for more entertaining responses:

What is your favorite condiment?

Who has had the most destructive influence on your life? Did you press charges?

If you could have dinner with any one person—historical or current, factual or fictitious, living or dead—what would you order?

Discuss a risk you took that involved pinching someone's butt.

Describe a national, regional, or local issue that you couldn't care less about.

Think about a cause that you're passionate about—but please spare us from hearing about it.

I Wear Adult Diapers: The Importance of an Effective First Line

Don't give admissions officers any excuse to put down your essay—grab them immediately with a compelling opening sentence. You don't have the luxury of building up to the good stuff a few sentences (or paragraphs) in. A powerful opening line doesn't have to be shocking, funny, or chock-full of SAT vocabulary words you memorized the night before—it just has to push the reader forward. A strong first line will create a sense of excitement, interest, and anticipation in the reader, motivating him or her to actually read the entire essay.

The essay is a vehicle for you to give a group of complete strangers a little insight into your personality. Helpful hint: make sure you have one. Although the questions may be somewhat contrived and disconnected from reality, admissions officers are really just trying to get a sense of who you are. Keep that underlying goal in mind as you're writing page 300 of your autobiography or describing which historical figure you'd love to have dinner with. Don't make your essay generic or impersonal.

"Put thought into your essays," says an admissions officer from Boston University. "I get really annoyed if I read an essay that says 'I want to go to BU because of Fenway Park, Boston Commons, shopping'—it's that universal answer that could be applied to any school." While you want your essay to be thoughtful and personal, don't attempt to convey *all* of your hopes, dreams, fears, aspirations, and perverted fantasies. You can't. Words are powerful, but they can't capture the sum total of a person. You should aim to communicate a small slice of yourself. Whatever the slice is, make sure it's riveting, interesting, and most important—you.

Have a Message

There is always a message embedded in your essay. Make sure you are keenly aware of the underlying point you want to convey, and use your essay as the medium for expressing it. If you write about a challenge you've overcome, what are you trying to tell an admissions committee? That you are resilient? That you seek challenging experiences? If you aren't clear on your message, this will come across in your essay.

Having a consistent message shows the admissions committee that you've not only thought carefully about the particular experience or issue but also learned something from it. Your message doesn't need to be a pivotal revelation or deeply insightful—it just needs a measure of self-awareness and introspection. See the essays at the end of this chapter for examples of effective messages.

Make the School Feel Special

Colleges are insecure; they want to know you want them. If admissions officers get the impression that they're only one of thirty-two schools you're applying to, they will not look favorably at your application, despite your stellar stats. Be mindful of how sensitive admissions officers are to your interest in their school and use your essay as an effective tool to demonstrate that interest.

Colleges also want to make sure that you will add something to the school. While that "something" is very subjective, you must communicate through your essay that *you will enrich the school and the school will enrich you*. Admissions officers are looking for a symbiotic relationship. They want to know that you will take full advantage of the school's resources (including free yogurt in the cafeteria) and that you have certain qualities that will add to the overall character of the student body.

Therein lies the secret at the heart of college admissions: you will never know exactly what traits you must possess to "add" to the school. The best you can do is to make your essay an extension of yourself and communicate that you are an interesting person, not merely an entity defined by scores and statistics. And if you don't have genuine interest in the school, then obey the credo that females have been living by for millennia: if you don't feel it, fake it.

The following chart will help you use your essay to communicate what you *really* want to tell colleges in a constructive way.

What You Want to Tell Colleges	How to Include That in Your Essay
Even though my grades suck, I think I'd be really happy at your school.	Discuss how you will rise to the occasion and reveal other dimensions that will make you an asset to the university.
I may be a grade-obsessed nerd, but I did go to a party once.	It's okay to be honest here—talk about why you value grades and work hard and how these traits will make you a great addition to the school.
I want to go to your school more than anything—I think it would be a great fit for my personality.	Be specific. Describe why the school appeals to you and how these reasons tie in with who you are.
I'm a snob. The prestige of your school matters to me.	Do not write this. Harvard knows you're not applying because of the succulent meatloaf in the cafeteria. Instead, elaborate on how *you* will enrich the school.
I'm smarter than most of your applicants and deserve to go to your college.	Again, do not write this. Talk about how your intellectual abilities will strengthen the school.

What You Want to Tell Colleges	How to Include That in Your Essay
You are my safety school, but I'm not sure how to say this without hurting your feelings.	The admissions committee knows this, but you are still required to summon some enthusiasm for the school. Do not express a holier-than-thou attitude in your essay. You never know when you'll need your safety school.
I'm applying because my guidance counselor told me to.	Stop right there and reread chapter 4.

Effective Essays by Real Students

The following are actual essays written by high school students who are now in college. The essays do a great job of revealing who the applicants are by combining storytelling, thoughtful reflection, and an insightful message. Most important, the authors describe how a challenging event became a meaningful, transformative experience.

Essay 1
Prompt: Evaluate a significant experience
you have faced and its impact on you.

> The Maori woman boarded the bus and instructed us on the proper way to greet the Chief. Thirty of us—all rising high school freshmen—walked off the bus confused. "What kind of culture requires students to greet their leaders with a kiss on both cheeks?" I wondered. I soon found out: the native New Zealand Maori did. It was the summer of 2006 and I was thousands of miles away from home on a People to People Student Ambassador Program for three weeks. It was the final week, and my group was staying in an authentic Maori hut for one night. My friends and I thought the stay

would be easy because New Zealanders spoke English. We were wrong.

Upon entering a long and narrow one-room building with a high-pitched roof carved with elaborate details, I saw the Chief and other natives waiting at the opposite end. We students waited in line and took our turns quickly and bashfully kissing the Chief. Once the greeting ceremony was complete, he began to speak. But I couldn't understand a word. Did I miss a memo to study this language? No English? The students all looked at each other more and more confused. At that point I realized this evening was not going to be an easy one.

I was very interested in learning about other cultures, and where better to learn than on an authentic Maori overnight stay? But how could I absorb their customs if I couldn't understand a word of what the man was saying? I realized I had to find another way to communicate.

I started to look more closely at the Chief while he spoke instead of simply focusing on what he was saying (Not hard to do, since I had no clue what he was saying . . .) I could see that he was using different hand motions and varied expressions on his face. From those slight changes in his body language, I began to understand more and more of what he was trying to convey to the group. Although I did not know *exactly* what he was saying, his actions and wide range of emotions spoke loudly enough.

That night, I learned a valuable lesson about how to communicate with someone. Effective communication is not just words; instead, communication also consists of actions and emotions that lie beneath those words, that give depth and nuance to those words. It's almost as if you could turn down the volume on people and still understand the story they are telling.

As I walked back onto the bus the next morning, I looked back and knew I had learned a valuable

> lesson—one that would change my thought process
> when developing story ideas and script writing for tele-
> vision production. Perhaps my life was influenced more
> by that night than I ever realized . . .

This author's underlying message—that she is a receptive person who thinks of creative ways to overcome challenges—is expressed nicely in this essay. The author also reveals herself to be resourceful: she looked for another way to understand the Chief when she realized traditional communication wasn't going to work.

This is a concise essay that not only answers the question but does so by telling an interesting story that successfully conveys what she wants to say. We understand that she faced a challenge, that she used her wits to overcome the challenge, and that the challenge influenced her perspective on communication. The concluding paragraph wraps everything up neatly by letting the reader know the experience's lasting impact on the author.

This essay is not earth-shattering; it describes the author's encounter with people of a foreign culture. We appreciate how she develops a deeper understanding about communication— a new awareness that it exists beyond words. Note the transition in the essay: the author is at first frustrated with her situation but quickly adapts and learns a lesson. While crafting your own essay, keep in mind that a transition or journey, regardless of how small, strengthens your essay. If you can write about how you changed or learned something new instead of merely describing an experience, your essay will be far more impressive. You'll demonstrate your maturity and ability to grow as a person.

Essay 2
Prompt: **Write an essay that conveys
to the reader a sense of who you are.**

I was in Japan, standing in front of the cramped classroom full of familiar faces gazing at me with curiosity.
"Unfortunately, Rebecca is leaving us . . ." I watched
my third grade classmates draw their breath. "Don't
worry, she will join her family in the United States and
make lots of new friends there!" The words echoed in
my ears as I stared uneasily at the gawking faces of my
stunned classmates.

"You're very excited, aren't you, Rebecca?" my
teacher asked. "Well . . ." I avoided answering the
question and forced a broken smile instead. In a way,
I *was* excited. However, no matter how hard I tried
to maintain a positive outlook, I could not ignore the
unsettling sensation in the pit of my stomach. Despite
my trepidation, I told my friends that I would write to
them every day, and that I would never forget Japa-
nese. At the end of class, they filed out of the room
dropping neatly written letters bursting with their
favorite stickers in my hands. I swallowed my tears
and managed to thank every single one of them.

Stepping into the plane heading to New York the
next day, warm tears streamed down my face, as I was
hit with the sudden realization that I would be leaving behind what I perceived as a perfect life. I recalled
my joyful memories of trading trendy stickers with my
closest friends, making "pretend soup" out of cherry
blossom petals and water at the local park, and riding
my tiny yellow unicycle around the familiar neighborhood. Tears rolled down faster and I struggled to stay
seated as the plane gained speed and lifted my body
from home.

As expected, America was nothing like Japan. I
was no longer in the familiar cramped classroom but in
a New York City public elementary school. Everything

was in English, which I soon realized was a major dilemma, as I only knew a maximum of ten words in English. The dramatic contrast in the two languages overwhelmed my nine-year-old brain. Like any other helpless child, I reached out to my mother, who tried her hardest to help me, but I soon realized that she was struggling too. The frustration caused me to lash out at her, demanding to know why we came here in the first place or why my father was not alive to help me. Instead of babying me, my mother forced me to snap to my senses and told me that I cannot think that way and promised me that it would be worth it in the end.

I constantly received cold stares from classmates who at first tried to be friendly to me, but finally gave up and labeled me as "the weird girl" because the answers to all of the questions they asked me was a nod or a shake of my head—even to questions such as "When is your birthday?" On the board, all I saw was a horde of alphabetical letters jumbled together. It took me twice the amount of time to copy the teacher's notes as regular students because while everyone copied words, I copied letters. During lunch hours, I made sure to hide my face behind my lunch box as I ate the rice balls my mother packed for me because I feared it would attract negative attention. One time, when I failed to cover my food, I overheard a girl whisper to her friend that I was eating "spider legs." Although I wanted so badly to tell her that it was simply seaweed that I was eating, I did not know how to put my ideas into words, and eventually gave up on my defense. As much as I desired some sort of social contact, I also tried as much as possible to avoid being asked questions because I knew I could not understand—let alone answer them.

Tired from the loneliness and isolation I felt on a daily basis, my biggest ambition became learning English. I knew that learning the language would solve all of my problems: I would be able to communicate

and meet new friends and tell them my birthday and
how school was like in Japan and what I was eating for
lunch. I wanted to prove to them that I was not weird
or quiet. Keeping this in mind, I dedicated all of my
time to conquering the language. As frustrated as I
was with the lingo, I took my mother's advice and told
myself that I would never give up.

Of course, "not giving up" was easier said than
done. I had days of meltdowns and outbursts, but I
slowly began to catch on. The sideways glances from
classmates became less frequent as I began to bravely
defend myself from the occasional taunts. My skills
in English eventually surpassed those of many of my
classmates because I spent so much time absorbing
the language.

Now, almost nine years later, I not only fully com-
prehend English but appreciate its intricacy. When I
was nine years old and struggling to learn a simple
sentence, it never occurred to me that I would become
a reporter for the high school paper, or that I would be
interpreting texts by Plato. If I have the ability to move
forward and surpass my own expectations, I believe
I have the willpower to further pursue the study of
English and continue this life-long quest in discovering
and unraveling the complexities of the most beautiful
language in the world.

This is a great example of an essay that illustrates how the
author successfully overcame obstacles. She faces a monumental challenge: to assimilate into American life without know-
ing the language. She writes beautifully about how she met
and even exceeded her goal of learning English. The author's
journey, from a nine-year-old immigrant to an accomplished
student of English, is told in vivid and concrete details, which
convey how difficult it was for her to adapt to her new life. The
author takes the bull by the horns, figures out how to solve her
problem, and recounts her determination to achieve a goal.

Another powerful element of the essay is how it leaves the reader wanting more: we're curious to see what lies in store for this brave, ambitious young woman. If you can accomplish this, you have done your job. Make your essay intriguing so that the reader (or fatigued admissions officer) wants to find out what happens next.

Essay 3
Prompt: Discuss your greatest accomplishment thus far.

I sat in silence with the other rebels of Chica Chica, a small Central American nation that no one has ever heard of. I had gone to Chica Chica on vacation with my family and decided to stay when I realized how badly the rebels needed me. I told my family I'd meet them in the U.S. after I finished leading the indigenous rebels to victory over their oppressive dictator, Juan Carlos Venezia de Mendez de Miranda Garcia, or "Chuck" for short.

It was astonishing to see how poor the people of Chica Chica were; they subsisted mainly on bananas and pebbles. I suggested they try putting salt on the pebbles (as I often do to my lox and bagels back home), but this suggestion was dismissed immediately. The rebels were too focused on their mission for such embellishments.

When I was asked to lead the rebel alliance, I had two choices: a) I could lead an oppressed people to taste the sweetness of freedom for the first time in their lives or b) I could go back home and catch up on "90210." The choice was clear: I told my mom to TIVO the episodes.

It was a difficult battle, fought with blood, sweat, and water guns. There were days when I wanted to give up because I just didn't think we could do it. As the leader, I often sat in my hotel suite while the rebels were out in the battlefields, just like George Washington did. In fact, I often quoted George as a way of inspiring the troops. His most famous quote: "These people suck, let's nuke 'em" seemed to work wonders in galvanizing the fatigued rebels.

But we were still losing. The evil dictator was on the brink of declaring victory when I decided to get out of the hot tub and check out what was going on in the field. It was the same old fighting, nothing new, so I popped back into the hotel. But something extraordinary had happened.

The rebels told me in broken English that during my brief sojourn out of my room, I had dropped a banana peel (I became obsessed with bananas and often ate six to eight a day), which Juan Carlos Venezia de Mendez de Miranda Garcia happened to slip on. He was rushed to the hospital and pronounced dead on the spot.

I am told they erected a statue of me in the town center. Although the inscription reads, "Never Underestimate the Power of an Idiot," I am flattered that I enabled thousands of people to break free from their shackles and embrace the bosom of freedom. I took on the challenge of saving a small country not because I was hoping this would help me get into college, but because I am genuinely concerned with the welfare of thousands of people whom I never met before and will probably never see again.

Gotcha! Yes, this essay is a fake—but believe me, some of the essays I've read that focus on students' "heroic" deeds are not that far off. If your essay even remotely resembles this one, rip up the paper and start again.

CHAPTER 10

The College Interview: Fourteen Ways Not to Screw It Up

The main goal of the college interview is to give the school a stronger feel for the real, live, in-the-flesh applicant. This is your chance to show the college who you really are. Use the interview to explain or elaborate on any information in your application: for instance, why your grades dipped in a particular semester or why you think you'd be a great fit at the school. The importance of the interview varies from school to school, but doing well can only strengthen your application.

As an alumni interviewer, I can give you some insider tips on how to ace your interview. If you follow the rules in this chapter, you are guaranteed to make a stellar impression.

1. Be Ready for Inescapable Questions

There are a handful of questions that almost every interviewer asks. Most of them will be clichés and repeat something you already answered on your application. You must respond with enthusiasm and pretend you love telling strangers about your greatest weaknesses. Do not shove a copy of your application in your interviewer's face and say, "It's all here—duh!" Instead, recite your prepared, memorized answers as if they were fresh, spontaneous thoughts. The chart below contains some of the most frequently asked questions, as well as answers that will cause your interviewer to slowly inch her chair away from you.

Interviewer's Question	Wrong Response
Why do you want to go to this school?	'Cuz it's better than bagging groceries.
Tell me something about yourself that's not in your application.	When I'm really nervous, I get pimples on my butt.
Tell me about a challenge you overcame.	I once had trouble opening a beer bottle so I used my teeth.
In one word, how would your family and friends describe you?	Smelly.
Where do you see yourself in ten years?	Celebrating my high school graduation.
Who in your life has most influenced you?	Yoda.

Finally, if you don't know the answer to a question, don't BS. It's better to say, "I don't know" than make something up and worsen the situation. You'll get extra points for honesty.

2. Improve Your Speaking Style

Unless you, like, um, you know . . . really want to kind of sound . . . like . . . kind of like an airhead, *omit the "likes," "ums," and "you knows" from your conversation.* No matter how qualified you are, peppering your discourse with these fillers has the same effect as wearing a backwards baseball cap: you'll just look stupid.

You're a teenager; of course you have verbal crutches. (Do you know anyone over forty who says the word "like" obsessively?) However, using "like," "um," and "you know" five times in a sentence can be a dangerous habit in the college interview. It's distracting and can send a false signal to the interviewer that you aren't prepared or aren't taking the interview seriously.

Be aware of your style of speech and try to speak in clean, clear sentences. The best way to prepare for the interview is to *practice*. I know, you've never heard that one before, right? But it's true. You have a good idea of what the interview questions will be. Sit down with a friend, teacher, parent, or other relative and practice your answers to basic questions. This exercise will not only help you devise solid answers but also sharpen your style of speaking. Make sure that style does not include profanity or spitting.

Here are some more speaking style tips to practice and keep in mind for the interview:

- ✔ Don't launch into your answer before thinking about it first; an artful pause is acceptable during the interview. (A two-hour nap is not.)

- ✔ Don't worry about cramming "big words" into a sentence. It's better to express your thoughts in plain, natural language than obfuscate your discourse by trenchant yet fatuous comments that lead ineluctably to a remonstrative end. Get it?

- ✔ Speak slowly. You don't want to drag out the interview to three hours, but be sure not to rush your answers.

3. Don't Be Late

Whether you're meeting an admissions officer, a volunteer alumnus (which will most likely be the case), or the president of the university, arrive on time. It's inconsiderate in general to keep someone waiting, and volunteer alumni are especially sensitive about their time (remember, they don't get paid for this). If you are running late, you better have a good excuse. (A hand-written note from Mommy and natural disasters won't cut it.) Whenever possible, call the interviewer to let her know when you'll walk your disgraced self through the door.

4. Connect with Your Interviewer

"I enjoy it when a student tries to connect with me personally," says Bill, an alumni interviewer from the University of Pennsylvania. "It's nice when a student asks me what I do for a living and what I thought of Penn." Even though *you're* the one being grilled like a burger patty on the fourth of July, it's important to make an effort to get the interviewer to talk about himself. You will definitely endear yourself to him if you take the time to try to bond over something.

To establish a good connection with your interviewer, you don't have to both love shih tzus, the color green, and sci-fi romances— you just have to find a subject that appeals to your interviewer and be able to talk about it. "My interviewer said she was a soap opera writer," says Jenn, a high school senior from Charlotte, North Carolina. "I never watch soaps, but I had just read an article about how *Guiding Light* was being canceled after seventy years, and I mentioned it to her. She seemed really excited that I knew that, and we talked about soaps for the next fifteen minutes." Jenn made a really good move. Even though in Jenn's opinion soaps are the entertainment equivalent of pond scum, she had the right instinct in mentioning something of interest to her interviewer. Jenn told me that the interviewer not only enjoyed discussing that specific topic but was in a good frame of mind for the rest of the interview.

If you go outside the boundaries by trying to connect with your interviewer rather than simply answering questions, you'll be far more likeable. I am always more inclined to like an applicant who takes the time to notice something about me and uses that as a way of drawing me out. It's perfectly fine to make an observation about the interviewer and allow her to expound—as long as you don't comment, "You have spinach in your teeth—did you brush today?"

Glenn from Newton, Massachusetts, noticed that his interviewer, an admissions officer for the school, had a poster of Barcelona in his office. Glenn, who had never been to Barcelona, simply asked him if he had traveled there. The admissions officer said he had been to Barcelona several times and that it was one of his favorite cities. "It was a good way of breaking the ice, and I think it made me feel less nervous when the meaty questions were thrown at me," says Glenn.

There are always opportunities for you to pipe up and forge a connection—it's just a matter of recognizing them. For example, if the interviewer makes an innocuous comment such as "Sorry I'm late, but I had to pick up my kids from ice hockey practice," ask how old the kids are. How long have they been playing ice hockey? Do they like it? Why do all ice hockey goalies look like Hannibal Lecter? It doesn't matter what you say as long as you attempt to make the interview more than a police interrogation.

5. Be Respectful

Don't ask your interviewer why she has nothing better to do with her free time than engage in boring, forced exchanges with high school students. There are many reasons alumni conduct interviews: it gives them a sense of pride to give back to their college, allows them to connect with college applicants, and provides a convenient timeout from their dysfunctional marriage.

Be gracious, thank the interviewer for her time, and get her email address so you can send a thank-you note the next day. Leave with a firm handshake (and the interviewer's wallet).

6. Sell Yourself

Just as you did in your essay, use the interview to link your interests to the college's resources and programs. Let the interviewer know that you plan to take full advantage of what the college has to offer. This is not the time to be coy; tell the interviewer that you can envision yourself at the school. If possible, embellish with relevant stories that underscore your devotion to the school or your strength as a candidate.

One alumni interviewer from Columbia interviewed a candidate who described how he scored a key Model UN position by incorporating one of the college's traditions into his tryout. The story not only demonstrated the candidate's initiative and leadership but also indicated to the interviewer how much he liked the school. The more lively and engaging you are, the more smoothly the interview will go and the more it will work in your favor.

7. Appear Interested

If you overtly check your watch during the interview, the interviewer may contemplate slapping you. You may be bored with the conversation, but don't make it obvious. Try to appear interested and engaged. It's not a good idea to dig an underground tunnel for a quick escape route.

8. Ask Questions About the School

Do some research beforehand and come prepared with specific questions about the college. Make sure they're not along the lines of "What school is this again?" It reflects poorly on you if you don't ask the interviewer questions, because that's generally read as a sign that you're not interested in the school. Here's where your research comes in handy: if you're thinking about being an English major, mention that you love the college's English class offerings. If you follow the football team's victories and losses, bring that up. Just like on the essay, this is a chance to link your interests with the school's resources, demonstrate that you'll gain something valuable from attending the school, and discuss how you'll contribute to enriching the community.

9. Avoid Excessive Eye Contact

Interviewers know you've been told to make eye contact, but don't stare as if the interviewer has a goiter. If you give the impression that your eyes will project laser beams at any moment, look away briefly—you're being too intense. As hard as it is, try to relax and pretend the interview is a conversation with your friend—make it conversational. It also helps if you can smile and even manage a laugh at some point.

10. Don't Get Too Personal

The interviewer may seem sympathetic, but she really doesn't want to hear about why you broke up with your boyfriend. Or that your rash makes it hard to urinate. Keep personal matters to yourself and focus on the questions. Also keep in mind that the interviewer is not an academic advisor. I've had students

ask me which classes they could drop without "looking bad."
I don't know how to answer this, and it puts me on the spot.

11. Answer with More Than One Syllable

This is possibly the most important rule of all. *talk.* Don't
answer just "yes" or "no" to questions like "Do you like to
read?" Elaborate—don't clam up and force the interviewer to
pry answers out of you as if removing your wisdom teeth. Your
job is to make the interview a pleasurable experience for the
interviewer. If the interviewer has a good time and enjoys your
conversation, you'll get a positive evaluation. If the interviewer
must rack his brain for things to say to fill the awkward silence,
that won't reflect well on you. (Some interviewers don't have
the patience to coax you into speaking, so they'll end the interview abruptly. You want to avoid this at all costs.)

12. Don't Recite Numbers

Refrain from bringing up your test scores or transcript. The
interviewer isn't there to pat you on the back for your 2300 SAT
score, nor is he there to rub it in if you failed gym—he's there
to pretend there is another dimension to your personality. The
interview is the one aspect of your application that allows you
to emerge from the veil of numbers and scores and transmit a
spark of your genuine personality.

13. Keep the Conversation Going

You won't hit it off with every interviewer—sometimes you'll
be at a loss for what to say and there will be an uncomfortable
silence. Maybe the chemistry isn't right, maybe you've exhausted
the usual topics but the interview isn't quite over. You can fake

an acute attack of appendicitis, but a better way to fill the conversation hole is to ask the interviewer questions. If you've done that already, ask more questions. Make sure, however, not to ask things like, "Where is New York University located again?" You may have to think on your feet for this one.

14. Don't Count on Freeloading

If you meet your interviewer at a café or coffeehouse, do not shove the bill toward him and say, "Thanks!" Hopefully the interviewer isn't a cheapskate and you'll get a free mochaccino out of the deal, but don't count on it. Even if the interviewer does intend to pay, he'll find it off-putting if you just assume he will. A good rule of thumb is to meet at a library or other neutral space that doesn't involve the exchange of money or drinks that could potentially leave a foam moustache. If you do find yourself at Cup o' Joe, offer to pay for yourself.

To Interview or Not to Interview?

Some schools require the interview as part of your application; others make it an optional step. Many students find the choice of whether or not to interview as stressful as the interview itself. If you don't interview, will you look like an antisocial recluse or like you're hiding something? If you do interview and mess up, will that look worse than if you just hadn't interviewed? There are certain cases in which it will definitely behoove you to set up an interview; likewise, there are certain cases in which you should just stay home and look up what *behoove* means.

When You Should Interview

✔ You would like to explain something on your record.

✔ You have a good personality and shower daily

✔ You mother dragged you by the ear to Starbucks, where the interviewer is waiting.

When You Shouldn't Interview

✘ You foam at the mouth when nervous.

✘ You are shy and introverted and know that you wouldn't project your best self in an interview.

✘ You only speak Swahili.

Ultimately, after you've read all the tips, practiced them, and written them in teeny type all over your left palm, you're going to have to trust yourself—you can handle this interview. Having confidence is half the battle; the other half is slipping a sedative into the interviewer's drink and writing the evaluation yourself.

CHAPTER 11

Things That Annoy Admissions Officers

There's a saying that dates back to the ancient Greeks: "Those who can't get a real job become admissions officers." Working in admissions at Plato's Academy was the equivalent of being a gym teacher today. In the twenty-first century, admissions officers garner a lot more respect than their archaic peers—mainly because they don't have to wear togas. Although the job can be high-pressure at times, being an admissions officer has its share of perks: free pens from college fairs, preferential treatment at campus cafeterias, and wielding power over thousands of strangers' lives.

What Admissions Officers Hate

You have probably figured out by now that you're not applying to a college or university, but an admissions committee. It's you against twelve to fifteen overstressed admissions officers who haven't seen their families in weeks because they're holed up in a dingy office reading your application and countless others. And that's the high point; they also travel around the country for months on end to answer the same questions over and over from overwrought students and parents: "Yes, we accept the ACT. No, we don't have a human sexuality major. Yes, we require three essays. No, parents cannot install Nannycam in their child's dorm room." It's very important that you—and your parents—do not piss these people off. So you need to know the six basic behaviors that are guaranteed to annoy admissions officers.

1. Emailing Obsessively

The first sin is probably the most widely committed in the Western world. It's fine to send admissions officers a follow-up thank-you note if they've taken the time to answer your questions. They like to see this, as it indicates interest in the school. But stop after an email or two—avoid clogging up their inbox. You don't want your email correspondence to resemble the following:

> Hi, thank you so much for meeting with me and answering my questions.
>
> Hi, did you get my email about the thank you? Anyway, thank you again.
>
> I haven't heard back from you—guess you're really busy.
>
> Are you traveling? I went to your house and peeked through your bedroom window but didn't see you.
>
> How come you're not picking up any of my phone calls? I've tried all five numbers.
>
> Please tell your wife I didn't mean to scare her. You should really get an alarm system.
>
> I tattooed your name on my left shoulder blade.
>
> Would you like to come over some time for boiled rabbit?

Admissions officers have enough on their plate. They don't have time to read—let alone answer—all the anxious queries they get. So choose your emails wisely and make them concise.

And *never* allow your parents to email, call, or manage your relationship with an admissions officer. The unanimous opinion is that parental interference will reflect horribly on you and likely cause uncomfortable situations.

"Sometimes a parent puts down her email on the application where the student is supposed to sign," says an admissions officer from a private school in upstate New York. "So I'm emailing the 'kid' when I know it's the parent, and it's very awkward." Students are much better off taking charge when it comes to contacting the admissions office. As Andrew Flagel, dean of admissions and enrollment at George Mason University, says, "Students will get more traction advocating themselves." Bottom line: If you no longer use a sippy cup, you don't need your parents to handle this stuff for you.

2. Calling an Admissions Officer

Unless the admissions officer gave birth to you, don't call. Admissions officers are really, really busy. They barely have time to answer your email, let alone start chatting on the phone. As anxious as you are for a response—any response—refrain from picking up the phone. Calling will certainly help you make an impression, but not the kind you want.

3. Submitting Too Many Letters of Recommendation

Your application is hard enough to get through; don't weigh these poor people down with a letter of recommendation from your childhood nanny. Accolades like "Joey burped beautifully" are not of interest to them. The majority of admissions officers I spoke with confirmed that two or three letters of recommendation (from your teachers) are perfectly sufficient. While it's tempting to submit a letter from everyone who has ever known and loved you, it's unnecessary and will be viewed in a negative light.

Some schools are asking parents to write a recommendation for their child. In that case, a letter from Mom or Dad is fine. The key word is *solicited*. If the application doesn't ask for it, don't submit a letter from the people who created you.

4. Writing Too Much

It's not going to impress anyone if you can't fit everything onto your application in the space provided. Although it's impossible to condense eighteen years of your life into a few pages, resist the urge to spill over onto attachments. Admissions officers take an average of fifteen minutes to go over your application; do not refer them to the napkin fragment that contains your excess thoughts. Be pithy and concise.

5. Including Too Much Supplemental Information

Unless the supplemental information truly adds significant value to your application, don't submit any. Some parents "send in every award the kid has ever won since nursery school, which weighs down the application," says a private college counselor. Of course, if you do have an extraordinary talent or ability, then it's acceptable to submit an example to the admissions committee. "If you're a great artist, then we need to evaluate your talent," says Marilyn McGrath Lewis, director of Harvard's undergraduate admissions. But don't go too far. Ms. Lewis recalls an instance in which a student sent the admissions office a sample of pie. Then the pies kept coming. "It didn't hurt his application, but it was unnecessary," she says.

Think before you submit—you don't want your supplemental information to overshadow the main aspects of your application. So if you're contemplating sending in a video of your dance recital from middle school, remember that even your parents can't endure that one. Ditto for any poetry that is reminiscent of Dr. Seuss.

6. *Stalking*

This is not acceptable or beneficial under any circumstances. If you know the admission officer's home address, license plate number, and real hair color, you know too much. If you want to get in, *don't stalk the admissions officer*.

What Admissions Officers Love

There are also certain behaviors that can make a positive impression on an admissions officer and increase your competitive edge. The following strategies will work in your favor, so capitalize on as many of them as possible.

1. *Attend College Fairs*

College fairs are a great opportunity to make contact with admissions officers. They do remember these events and take note of students who inquire about the school. Also, if representatives of schools you're interested in come to your high school, try to meet with them one-on-one or in a small group.

2. *Make a Good Impression*

If you're meeting with a representative of a school you're interested in, there are small steps you can take that will add up to a positive impression. Keep the following suggestions in mind during these exchanges:

- ✔ Always be polite and cheery. No one wants to let in a Debby Downer.
- ✔ Keep your interactions brief. If you hog all the admissions officers' time at college fairs or at your high school, they won't have time to answer other students' questions. They *will* remember your self-serving assertiveness.

✔ Be positive about the school. Even if your feelings are obvious to you, they won't obvious to others unless you express them. Let the admissions officers know you want to attend their school. Be wary of being *too* enthusiastic, though. Statements like "My first word was *Harvard*" and "I have U Michigan panties" are not positive—they're scary.

✔ Keep your parents under control. Again, balance is the key. It's fine for your parents to accompany you to college fairs and ask questions, but make sure they don't overshadow you or take over the discussion.

✔ Do not dress up as the school's mascot.

✔ Take along breath mints. I have attended many a college fair where I had to take a few imperceptible steps back because someone's oral hygiene had fallen by the wayside. So please, pop a Tic Tac.

3. Ask Specific Questions

It's important that you make the most of your time with admissions officers to gain insights into the school. If you ask them a general question, you'll get a general answer. For example, if you ask, "Do you need good grades to get in here?" how do you expect the guy to respond? Even the admissions officers from You-Don't-Have-to-Be-Literate U will say, "Yes, you need good grades." So when you approach an admissions officer, make sure your questions are intelligent and specific to the school. Even though college fairs, visits to high schools, and information sessions are part of the exploratory stage of your search, asking questions that are addressed on the first page of the brochure is a surefire way to tick off an admissions officer.

Admissions officers encourage students to ask questions about the school that will help them make an informed choice about applying. "One student asked me if it's true that our students refuse to share notes with each other before exams," says an admissions officer from an Ivy League school. "I thought it was a completely valid question. If that student was under the impression that everyone at our school tries to sabotage each other, she's not going to get an accurate idea of what the school is about."

Karen from New York also asked a good question that helped her decide where to apply. "After I talked to a rep from a school on the West Coast, I decided I didn't want to go there," she says. "I asked him what students do for fun, and he told me that most students were very into outdoor activities. It just didn't seem to fit me—I'm not a skiing or hiking kind of person." Because hurtling down an icy slope or hauling herself up a rock face aren't Karen's idea of a good time, she reconsidered applying to that particular school.

Now a word of caution. When you ask your questions, you can't take everything an admissions officer tells you at face value. To some degree, admissions officers are also salespeople. It's their job to persuade you to want to attend their college. Regardless of whether you end up going there, they want you to apply and will therefore put the school in the best possible light. Most have a script to stick to, and very few are going to admit that every year over 90 percent of students transfer somewhere else. So whatever an admissions officer says to you, it's important to double-check the information with current students. College is a business that needs customers; unfortunately, you can't fully trust anyone in the admissions game.

Admissions officers are capable of putting a positive spin on pretty much anything. Some might even say that the only difference between admissions officers and used car salesmen is that a used car salesman doesn't care what you got on your SATs. To help you understand how admissions officers sometimes stretch the truth, here are examples of how they can spin absolutely anything.

Accurate Observation from Students and Parents (the Truth)	Admission Officer's Response (the Spin)
I heard that a few students died from meningitis last year.	Oh no, some students just fell asleep during class. They just haven't woken up yet.
Your school has a reputation for having an uptight and serious student body.	Our students are pretty laid-back; we just have a high suicide rate.
Someone said that multiculturalism isn't a big thing on campus.	Not true. All the white kids eat at Taco Bell.
We've been told you don't award generous financial aid packages.	We don't award any financial aid at all. But we do give out delicious chocolate-chip cookies in the admissions office.
We heard there's nothing to do at your school but drink.	There's also cow tipping.
Even with perfect grades and SAT scores, it's impossible to get into your school, right?	Not impossible. But yes, we are mainly recruiting students who are half human, half Cylon.

Remember to treat admissions officers with respect and they will do the same for you. Even though they see you as a few pieces of paper instead of a person, having a positive relationship with them will make the college application process much easier.

CHAPTER 12

How to Pass the Time While You're Waiting to Hear

As a wise man once said, "It's over, you obsessive freak." The applications are in, and there's nothing more you can do to convince the admissions committee to let you in. And stop checking the status of your application—they've already sent you an email confirming that they received it.

Most people would agree that one of the most brutal aspects of college admissions is the waiting. And the waiting. The long, agonizing days between January and April are sheer torture. For the first time in your life, you have no idea where you're going to be next year. Your usual sense of security and stability disintegrates as it becomes clear that wherever you wind up, your teddy bear won't be welcome. Aside from this staggering uncertainty, you face a huge dilemma: do you blow off the rest of senior year or continue to work at the same maniacal pace you've maintained for the past three and a half years? Obviously, neither extreme is good. You don't want to fail Acting, but you don't want to spend your weekends reading books like *Stimulate Yourself with Algorithms* for extra credit, either.

Healthy Ways to Spend the Limbo Period

Here are some suggestions for enjoyable activities and hobbies you can pursue over the coming months. Now that your future is entirely out of your hands, you'll need a few ways to pass the time.

Rediscover the Fun of Learning

You don't have to worry about getting a 99 instead of a 96 on your history exam anymore. So instead of inputting material into your head like a Vulcan, go at your own pace and take the time to truly digest the material.

Spend More Time with Friends

You can actually be social on weeknights now. Go on, go out to the local diner on a Wednesday night and enjoy some matzo ball soup and cheese fries with your friends.

Try Something Different

You don't have to impress colleges anymore, so stop researching the affects of the p53 derived peptide on pancreatic cancer growth and try an activity that really means something to you. Sign up for a yoga class, play Hacky Sack, or take up Brazilian fight-dancing. You've earned the right to do something that you never had time to do before.

Check Out a Newspaper

You may be surprised to learn that George W. Bush is no longer president. Reading the paper is a good habit to get into before college. Staying abreast of current events will help make you an informed, well-rounded individual. Plus, a copy of *The Times* may come in handy if you run out of toilet paper.

Read!

And I don't mean the magazines in the supermarket checkout line. If you've never had time to read *To Kill a Mockingbird*, *The Adventures of Huckleberry Finn*, *Anna Karenina*, *Pride and Prejudice*, or any other book longer than fifteen pages, now is the time. Reading will not only enrich and broaden your perspectives but also help strengthen the writing and comprehension skills you'll need for college. Don't wait until you're retired to pick up a book; you may have cataracts by then.

Ease Up—But Don't Give Up—on Studying

Moderation is key. Although you should definitely study during your second semester, don't feel compelled to maintain the same intensity you'd had up to this point. In other words, feel free to go to bed before three in the morning.

Unhealthy Ways to Spend the Limbo Period

There are also certain things that you should absolutely *not* do while you're waiting to hear from colleges. Avoid the following behaviors at all costs.

Reexamining Your Applications

Once you drop the envelope in the mailbox or press the "Send" key, it's over. I will put myself forward as an example of why it's extremely unhealthy to review your application after it's already in. Because I didn't have enough hobbies, I reread the essay I had written for my early decision application to UPenn. I discovered a fatal flaw that shattered my peace of mind and haunted me for the next few months: I had misspelled the word *innate* as *inate*, with one N instead of two. "My life," I thought, "is over."

I even approached my English teacher, who had kindly proofread my essay, and asked him how he could have missed the mistake. He laughed and said he was human. "You're not human," I said, furious. "You're a monster." Okay, I didn't really say that. But I was devastated. My teacher told me that if Penn would reject me on the basis of one misspelled word, then I didn't want to go there. I didn't know how to convey to him how badly I *did* want to go there. I was distraught for weeks—I had convinced myself that there was no way Penn would take me after such a glaring error.

In the end, I was accepted—and surprisingly, the acceptance letter didn't read: *We'll take you despite the fact that you're innately an idiot.* I had wasted so much precious time worrying for nothing. Of course it's easy to say this now, but if I hadn't gotten in, it would have been fine too. (Instead of writing books, I would have taken up a career in panhandling.) The point is, there was nothing I could do about the misspelled word. My application—like every application—was evaluated not on the accurate spelling of every single word, but on my strength as a potential student. It would have been much better for me to stop obsessing and just let fate take its course. Either that, or hope that the admissions officers were too inebriated to notice.

The applications are out of your hands. Rest assured that you have done everything you possibly could have to make the best case for yourself. So enjoy yourself—don't squander this time by thinking of things you should have done differently.

The other major lesson of the story is to (surprise, surprise) spell-check. But even spell-check can let you down. Even well-meaning English teachers can let you down. So read your essay carefully (both on the screen and on actual paper), ask a parent or teacher to take a look, then stop dwelling on it. There is no such thing as perfection in life, and there is no such thing as perfection in a college application.

Leaving School after Second Period

Unless your day consists of two periods, it's not a good idea to start cutting class in the second semester of your senior year. Many students feel they have "earned" the right to blow off school. This mind-set is perfectly understandable: you've worked like a dog to get to this point, and now you want a little R&R. Or maybe you didn't work like a dog, but you figure that with just a few months of high school left, it's not going to matter whether or not you show up for European History. But don't you want to find out who won World War II?

Whatever your reasons for an acute case of senioritis, you must summon all your strength and conquer it. Here are a few of the main reasons why you should not blow off classes at the end of high school:

> You might fail and not graduate.
>
> Your college acceptance might be retracted. Those threats from colleges are true: if there is a steep drop in your grades during your second semester, you might kiss that acceptance good-bye.
>
> It's flat-out lame. Unless you're doing something really cool—like scaling a skyscraper to save humanity from the Green Goblin—it's just silly to cut class. (Sorry, smoking a joint in the parking lot is not considered cool.)
>
> You're only cheating yourself. Corny, but true. You're depriving yourself of an education that you are entitled to. So don't blow off that Home Ec course; those sewing skills will come in handy at college when holes start appearing in your underwear in inconvenient places.

I hate to keep using myself as an example, but I'm going to anyway. After I got into Penn early decision, I was psyched. As a result, I was bitten very hard by the senioritis bug, which manifested itself most strongly in my AP Biology course. I ended the year getting a C in the class, and my teacher told me not to bother taking the AP Bio exam because I had put in absolutely no work for many months. The suggestion to not take the exam lit a fire in my belly—I was shocked and appalled that my biology teacher would even mention that as an option. Biology was my favorite subject, and up until my college acceptance, I had done well in it.

I studied for that exam day and night, and when the time came, I was prepared to take it. My efforts paid off, and I got college credit for the course. The impetus for studying so hard was my bio teacher's obvious loss of faith and respect for me. I was ashamed of myself for decaying into a bio bum. If I had it to do over again, I wouldn't have slacked off the way I did. Looking back, blowing off exams and papers didn't make me any happier. I knew I was doing something wrong, and I lost the sense of satisfaction that came with mastering the material. I will never forget how a fruit fly reproduces. And neither should you.

Recalculating Your GPA While Everyone Else Is at the Prom

Go to prom, and for goodness sake, get some action. Even if it's with your physics teacher who's chaperoning—you want something more exciting to happen on prom night than playing with the glass partition in the limo.

Grade Grubbing

What's the point of grade grubbing now? Even if you think you have a genuine case, let it go. Do you want to risk antagonizing your teachers to the point where they band together and beat you up with dry-erase markers and beakers in the parking lot after school?

Doing Anything for Extra Credit

You don't need extra credit anymore. Not only is the work time-consuming and unnecessary, but your teachers never actually thought you'd take them up on it. If you're that desperate for intellectual stimulation, contact your third grade teacher and find out whether you can resubmit your dinosaur diorama.

Spending Spring Break Helping People

You don't have to pretend you're a good person and do things like Habitat for Humanity anymore! So buy a plane ticket, go someplace with palm trees, and have fun with your friends—just don't end up on any spring break videos.

Drag Racing

If you need a high that badly, take a few sniffs of Wite-Out.

Smell the Roses

You may discover that you have more time on your hands now, so slow down and take it easy in your second semester. Once the unrelenting pressure of getting into college evaporates, you'll find that the air smells fresher, the sky is bluer, and that your hair is silky and shiny now that you have time to shower. If you do any of the following, you'll be on your way to enjoying the rest of high school:

Learn the name of your baby brother

Change your underwear for the first time since September

Take time to cook meat instead of eating it raw

Tell your imaginary girlfriend it's time to start seeing real people

Play on your swing set and scream, "Look at me!" when the swing goes really high

PART THREE

The Envelope Arrives: Whatever Happens, Don't Take It Out on the Mailman

It's not the mailman's—sorry, mail *carrier's*—fault if you were rejected from your first-choice college. If you were accepted to your dream college, then congratulations. If you weren't, take a deep breath and remain calm.

Although it may seem that applying to college is the hard part, the aftermath can be pretty tough too. Being rejected, figuring out where to go, financing your education, and considering whether to take time off are all difficult situations. To keep things in perspective, you can have one of two attitudes: "I was the victim of a heartless, haphazard admissions process that sucked the very marrow out of my soul" or "Things work out the way they do for a reason."

CHAPTER 13

Without Rejection, There'd Be No Ben & Jerry's

Face it, no one eats Ben & Jerry's because they're in a good mood. So let's take a moment of silence to praise the existence of rejection because without it, we wouldn't have "Half Baked." Still, even a pint of sugar-loaded comfort food can't completely cushion a harsh blow, like a college rejection letter. If you receive a thin envelope—especially one from one of your top schools—you'll probably be devastated, shocked, pissed off, or all of the above. Even though your emotions will be running high, keep in mind these key ground rules:

Do not ask the admissions committee why they rejected you.

Do not write to the admissions committee, "You'll pay for this someday."

Do not pretend you never got the letter and show up on campus the first day of school.

Do not resend your application under a different name the following year.

Remember that colleges aren't rejecting you—they're rejecting a few pieces of paper. So technically, they're rejecting paper.

There is no way to sugarcoat rejection. No matter how many times admissions officers assert that there were so many qualified applicants, it was such a tough decision, how they wish they could accept every single brilliant student, blah, blah, blah, they can never convince you that you were rejected because they liked you so darn much. The level of hurt you're feeling obviously depends on how badly you wanted to go to the school. If you were rejected by your top choice, you may be hibernating in your room for a while. If you didn't care about getting in, the sting should be less painful. But regardless of how much you wanted to attend a particular college, you certainly don't want to be told you can't come. Feeling lousy about rejection is normal. As a result, you're entitled to a few extra perks during this time, including:

✔ Unlimited access to your parents' car

✔ Permission to go out without calling every fifteen minutes to "check in"

✔ A new puppy

✔ A trust fund

Cope with Rejection

If these perks don't adequately ease your pain, there are other ways to overcome rejection. Here are some coping strategies to try out if you're faced with a dreaded thin envelope.

Let Time Heal You

Remember, this too shall pass. In a week, the sting will hurt a little less, in two weeks even less, and by next September you won't even remember where you got in and where you didn't. Unless you're the serial-killer type who hatches twisted plots in an isolated log cabin, you will move on with your life, and the hurt that you felt at first will fade into oblivion.

Remind Yourself "It's Their Loss"

This affirmation has never worked for anyone—not at first, anyway. But if you keep saying it to yourself enough times, it does become true. Okay, so they didn't want you. Who the hell are they? They don't know what they're missing. They're losing a lot more than you are. It's not you, it's them. Throw in any other cliché as needed to soften the blow.

Find Your Misery Some Company

Commiserate with other losers—I mean, other awesome people whose incredible qualities were also overlooked. Misery loves company. You know that you're not the only one who has ever been rejected by a college; actually talking about the experience with someone else in the same boat is pretty darn therapeutic.

Go Ahead, Brood

It's okay to dwell for a while. Allow yourself some time to obsess, sulk, vent—anything that will help you get the pain out of your system. Don't, however, indulge yourself too long. If you're still crying at your graduation ceremony, seek help.

Blame Someone Else

The best way to deal with rejection is to pass the blame onto an innocent bystander. Like the evil mailman, who could have opened your application and doused it in chocolate syrup. Or your guidance counselor, who could have sent the wrong paperwork. It's also not impossible that whoever cleans the admissions office just didn't like your name and tossed your application into the "Reject" pile. Or maybe your application got sucked into a time vortex and will arrive at the admissions office in thirty-five years.

Acknowledge Your Inadequacy

Realize that you're just not good enough. The admissions committee was obviously very insightful in detecting flaws in your character and deficiencies in your talents from just a few sheets of paper. You really aren't worthy of attending their school.

Do you see how ridiculous that sounds? In the end, no college can make you feel inferior without your consent.

Don't Take It Personally Unless the Letter Says "We Hate You"

It's natural to ask: Why didn't they take me? What was it about me that they didn't like? Very often, it's not about you at all. The process of choosing college applicants is like works of art, symphonies, and *Sports Illustrated* swimsuit models: it's extremely subjective. The "Admit" or "Reject" decision is usually based on the idiosyncrasies of the admissions officers handling your application. So when you are faced with a rejection letter, keep telling yourself that the admissions officers turned you down for one of the following top-secret reasons:

> We ask students to tell us what makes them "tick," but reject the ones who actually do.
>
> If there are two equally stupid applicants, we'll take the one who has more money.
>
> Selfless philanthropists = irritating, overachieving kiss-ups.
>
> Taking a "holistic admissions approach" really means that we reject boring white kids.
>
> We can't stand students who are smarter than us.
>
> The average temperature here is 20 degrees and most of the time we're in a bad mood.
>
> We have an "eeny, meeny, miny, moe" system, and only 10 percent of the applicants fall under "moe."

Decode Admissions-ese

College rejection letters tend to be nice and polite, which can make the sting of rejection even more painful. Admissions officers have mastered the art of couching the real reasons they reject you in their typical cryptic, euphemistic jargon. Want to know what "he wasn't a good fit" actually means? This handy chart decodes what those rascals are really saying.

Ostensible Reason for Rejection	Real Reason for Rejection
The applicant wasn't a good fit.	We were afraid you might blow up the school.
The student wouldn't thrive here.	We don't see you making any friends.
Her academic record didn't meet our standards.	News flash: We don't let in morons.
We had so many qualified applicants this year, it was impossible to choose.	Your SAT scores sucked.
The applicant would prosper in a different environment.	We looked you up on Facebook and, damn, you're ugly.
We didn't get the sense the student wanted to be here.	You should have used another college as your safety school, schmuck.

Wouldn't rejection be easier if the letter was vicious and nasty? That way, you would have much more justification for loathing the admissions officers. Rejection hurts no matter what, but it might hurt a little less if you received the following letter.

Dear Applicant,

We regret that we are unable to offer you a spot in next year's incoming freshman class. Not! It's actually quite titillating to reject annoying little overachievers such as yourself. The more you "challenged yourself" and the harder you worked, the more we hated you.

You should have gotten drunk more often in high school, because whatever you were doing was clearly a waste of time. Long story short, you had no friggin' chance at getting in here. The lucky few who were accepted got in only because the dean of admissions ordered us to "Pick the names out of the goddamn hat, already" two days before the letters were sent out.

Good luck with your future endeavors—we don't give a flying #*&$ where you end up.

Smoochies,
The Admissions Committee

P.S. This letter contains anthrax.

Why HPY Is an "AP" Away from Happy

If you were brave enough to apply to the golden triumvirate of HPY (Harvard, Princeton, and/or Yale), then chances are you didn't get in. On the bright side, you're in good company. With acceptance rates averaging around 7 percent, these Ivies reject some seventy thousand students a year who go on to live wretched lives and end up working in tollbooths. (Do you really believe that? Yeah, I didn't think so.)

Because these schools reject most of their applicants, you can't take it personally. And if you are rejected from the crème de la crème of higher education, keep the following in mind:

You'll always have an official letter from Harvard, even if it says, "We don't want you here."

Under the "Education" portion of your resume, you can write, "Almost Got into Yale."

You won't have to join their snooty alumni clubs and pretend you know how to smoke a cigar.

You can now freely refer to anyone who goes to HPY as a "freak."

You can put a metaphysical twist on the situation and say, "I rejected them."

If you're still dying to wear a Princeton sweatshirt, you can always apply there for grad school.

Rejection Stories

Everyone loves a good rejection story. Unfortunately, when it comes to college, there are no good rejection stories. Rejection is a cruel, heartless, joyless rite of passage that is part and parcel of college admissions. "It's worse than being dumped," says Jeffrey from Scottsdale, Arizona. "At least the girl says to you, 'Let's be friends.' The colleges basically never want to see you again."

There are some persistent applicants who won't take no for an answer. Caleb from Los Angeles, California, said that when he was rejected from an Ivy League school, he called the dean of admissions "every day the entire summer." Finally, the dean said to him, "If I let you in, will you stop harassing me?" Caleb said yes, and the dean responded, "I'm still not letting you in, but I will call the police if you don't stop calling." This convinced Caleb to put an end to his campaign for admittance.

There are thousands of ways to deal with rejection—some more offbeat than others. Sharon from Dix Hills, Long Island, actually hung the five rejection letters she received on the wall of her room. "It sounds bizarre; the more I stared at the letters, the more comical the whole thing was. It was so impersonal; it started to mean less and less. My friends kept asking me why I would want to see the rejection letters all the time, but after a few weeks I became numb to them. When my acceptance letters came, I taped them over the rejections and it was really cathartic."

It's also okay to shed a few tears. But try not to get carried away— don't let your grief about one school sour your acceptances from others. "I cried when I was rejected from Washington University," says Steve, now a junior at Yale. "I seriously hadn't cried since middle school, so my family was worried. I just felt like I had done all this work for four years for nothing. When I got into Yale, I was more subdued than I would have been because I was so upset over Wash U."

Anju from Bryn Mawr, Pennsylvania, was rejected by eight out of ten schools. "I looked at my two acceptances and could not believe that this is what my life came down to," she says. Anju had very little desire to attend either of the schools. "I wanted to hibernate for the rest of my life." But then she talked to other students in her class who were also rejected from their top choice schools. "You feel better when you realize you're not alone. There's kind of a secret elation you get when someone else is going through the same thing you are."

Get Excited About Where You Are Going

Dr. Jonathan Tobkes, a child and adolescent psychiatrist in New York City, says a good way to deal with rejection is to "direct your energies toward where you will most likely go to college rather than where you're not going." So instead of dwelling on your rejections, start thinking about your options and immerse yourself in the idea of attending those colleges. Dr. Tobkes says, "Your time is much better spent focusing on real possibilities and getting excited about those schools that have accepted you."

Matt from Westchester County, New York, was dead set on going to New York University. "When NYU rejected me, I didn't even want to think about another college," he says. He got an acceptance from the School of Visual Arts in New York City and wasn't interested. "So many people told me that everybody gets into SVA so it's not a big deal." But then Matt's older sister, who was also rejected from NYU and went to Emerson College in Boston, told him to give SVA a chance. "I spoke with other kids who were going to SVA and they were psyched about it. Then I started thinking, *If that's where everybody gets in, then I want to go where everybody is going.*" Matt is now a happy freshman who is so busy with activities that he rarely has time to call his sister and thank her for her good advice.

Dr. Tobkes points out that when you compare the number of people who are rejected from college (which is virtually everyone who applies) to the number of people who transfer colleges, the percentage of transfer students is relatively small. That information suggests that the vast majority of students are relatively happy where they end up, or else there would be an astronomical number of transfer students. "The bottom line is that if you embrace wherever you wind up going to school and give it a chance, you'll most likely wind up happy," says Dr. Tobkes.

CHAPTER 14

How to Choose the Right School (They All Look Good in Brochures)

"My parents hired a spiritual advisor to help me decide where to go," says Kelly from Santa Monica, California. "She told me that I would hate Stanford and that I should go to USC. I got into both and chose USC." Although listening to spiritual advisors, fortune cookies, or your four-year-old cousin may not be the best methods for choosing where to go to college, many students are hard pressed to come up with a better way.

"I got into five really good schools and had no idea where I wanted to go," says Danielle, a New York native and junior at Indiana University. "I kept changing my mind every five seconds and could not make a decision." Danielle and her mom went back to her top three schools for a final visit. When even that didn't help, she decided on the school that was farthest from home. "I realized that I wanted to live in a different part of the country because I'm going to come back to New York anyway," she explains. A student from Baldwin, New York, visited NYU a second time after she was accepted and saw a clear-cut sign that it was where she belonged: "I saw another freak in pink neon tights and knew I was home."

Picking a college feels like one of the biggest decisions of your life. Where to spend the next four years is not something to be taken lightly. However, the more weight you place on selecting the one "right" school, the more pressure you put on yourself and the more paralyzed you become about making a decision. Remind yourself that all colleges have the same goal: they want the students to be happy. Really. Higher education has become a competitive business; colleges and universities want as many clients (people like you) as possible, so they do their utmost do invest in high-quality facilities and faculty, barely edible food, and flushable toilets to make their school an appealing place. In other words, wherever you end up, you'll enjoy yourself. So don't expend too much energy stressing out about where to go—you've already had enough breakdowns during the admissions process.

That said, you shouldn't pick just *any* school to get this dilemma over with. Making the final choice does require some careful thought and research. Here are some suggestions to help you make a final decision:

- ✔ **Look at your notes from college tours.** Closely reexamine your original impressions. These initial feelings often stem from your gut reaction, which will almost infallibly lead you in the right direction.

- ✔ **Talk to as many current undergrads as you can.** If possible, expand your search beyond graduates of your high school; it's most helpful to speak with different kinds of people to get a broader sense of what the school is really like.

- ✔ **Go to Acceptance Days or Weekends.** Most schools have special days or weekends for accepted students to give them a taste of life on campus. Take advantage of these whenever possible, but be aware that every college goes all out to seem like an awesome place. This tradition is like that of law firms who wine and dine their summer associates, then once they're hired, lock them in dungeons for the rest of their lives.

✔ **Remember why you applied.** Maybe you've forgotten your reasons for applying in the first place. Reconnecting with your original goals can help clarify your thought process and give you some perspective. (Hopefully, your goals are a little more profound than "hooking up with hot cheerleaders.")

✔ **Think about your future.** You don't have to know exactly what you want to do with your life just yet, but you probably have some possibilities in mind. For instance, if you think you may want to be an actress, make sure the school has an acting program.

✔ **Focus on your desired location.** Do you crave an urban campus, rural campus, or suburban campus? A school in the arctic tundra, desert, or rainforest? Be true to yourself: if you love mountain biking and hiking in your free time, don't go to a school in a metropolis where the nearest tree is fifty miles away.

✔ **Stand by your decision.** Once May 1st rolls around, your life will be changed irrevocably. The next four years are permanently etched in the annals of eternity and are completely unalterable. *Just kidding!* Ever hear of transferring?

Wrong Reasons for Picking— or Not Picking—a College

Among the many valid reasons for choosing or declining a particular college, there are many poor ones. Do not, I repeat, do *not* base your decision on any of the following factors.

Pressure from Family and Friends

To make the very best choice, you must distance yourself from what your family and friends think. Your friend may encourage you to go to Duke because she's going to UNC. Your dad may love for you to go to Washington University because he went there. Although it's fine to seek guidance when figuring out where to go to college, make sure that the final decision comes from *you*. If you allow anyone else to have a major influence on your choice, then you are not going to a college for the right reasons.

This scenario is especially true for legacy applicants, the ones we love to hate. Often legacies apply to a particular school because of unrelenting parental pressure to do so. If they get in, they face even more pressure to attend. "My dad would not accept the fact that I did not want to go to Northwestern," says Jeff, a freshman at Columbia. Jeff explains that his dad was intent on continuing a family legacy that began with Jeff's grandfather. Although Jeff felt like he was ruining his father's dream, he was steadfast in his desire to attend Columbia. Whether or not you're a legacy, tell your parents to stop trying to live their dreams through you—otherwise, your therapy bills will cost more than four years at Harvard.

The Friendliness of the Tour Guide

One college graduate refused to even apply to Williams because the tour guide was "snooty." She says she later regretted that decision when she visited a friend at the school: "I totally saw myself there. It was stupid not to apply."

Your Boyfriend/Girlfriend or Best Friend Is Going

A college junior decided to attend Northeastern because her boyfriend was going there. "When we broke up at the end of freshman year, I was devastated—not only because we broke up, but because I didn't even like the school."

The Weather

Even if there's a blizzard or sandstorm when you tour the campus, don't jump to conclusions about the weather based on only one day. No one likes to see a college in the rain, but keep in mind that the weather won't be gloomy every single day; likewise, it won't always be sunny and 80 degrees. If you want perfect weather, you'll have to go back to the Garden of Eden.

The Food in the Dining Halls

Yes, food is important, but it's not a reason to say yea or nay to a school. Chances are that Rachael Ray isn't manning the kitchen, so the food might not be worthy of a four-star restaurant. Keep in mind that there are always other options, from local eateries to grocery stores to food trucks. If the on-campus grub isn't to your liking, you might even be motivated to learn how to cook, assuming your dorm has a kitchen. If it doesn't, invest in a hot plate, but avoid sitting on it.

The Prestige Factor

Yes, even the Ivies get chosen for the wrong reasons. If you've imagined painting a crimson "H" on your chest for the Harvard-Yale football game since you were six, then by all means enroll. But don't delude yourself into thinking that these schools will guarantee happiness or a successful career. Yes, there is something inherently cool about filling out Harvard, Princeton, or Yale on a job application, even to TJ Maxx. However, a Yale sophomore told me that he was disappointed in the quality of his education. "I take a lot of survey courses, and it's really hard to get one-on-one time with professors," he says. In fact, he admits that he thinks his high school education was actually better than the one he's currently receiving. And Michelle, who recently graduated from Harvard, confessed that she would have been happier at a more laidback school. "I found a lot of people to be really intense," she says. "I think I would have preferred a different kind of student body."

I'm not saying you can't be happy at an Ivy League school, but keep in mind that attending one may not be all it's cracked up to be. Plus, after you graduate, people get annoyed if you mention your alma mater too much. You won't win any friends with statements like, "Is it just me or does that butter patty look like the Yale bulldog?" or "I think it's going to rain today. That reminds me of the day it rained at Princeton."

Your Psychic's Input

Do I even have to get into this one?

Do Some Digging Online

When it comes to making a final decision, it definitely helps to hear what current undergrads are saying about their school. In addition to pulling aside random students when you're on campus, researching online is a great way to gather information. Check out the following websites, which provide student-generated feedback about schools:

- ✔ **Unigo** (www.unigo.com) enables high school students to read in-depth reviews of the schools they're interested in. College students offer a tremendous amount of insight (more than you'll find in all the college review books put together) and post videos and pictures to give prospective students a visual glimpse into life at their school. Unigo's subsearch feature allows you to generate a detailed, customized search. For example, you can read reviews of Tufts University by Asian females or reviews of every college in the country by left-wing students from Ohio. The site's social networking component allows you to connect with the reviewer and get in touch with other high school students who are considering the same school.

✔ **College Prowler** (www.collegeprowler.com) has great candid reviews from students, and it allows you to compare schools. Each college gets a report card with grades for its different aspects, such as campus housing, nightlife, and athletics. It's an excellent way to glean helpful information that you might not hear about on the tours.

✔ **Students Review** (www.studentsreview.com) has "uncensored" student reviews that can read like personal diary entries, giving you a true taste of what campus life is like. In addition to providing basic background information about colleges, the site ranks various dimensions of the schools, such as the social life and extracurricular activities.

Of course, you can't base your decision solely on student reviews. Although it is important to weigh current students' opinions about their school, you need to make up your own mind. Like choosing a good mechanic, at some point it's necessary to take a leap of faith and just make a decision.

Quiz: Choosing the College That Fits You Best

I know, you already took a suspiciously similar quiz in chapter 3, but this is a more refined version. It will help you narrow down your options to your final choice (or confuse you even more—in which case you should rip up this page).

1. Do your college choices include programs that you may be interested in pursuing?

    A) Maybe—I have no idea what I want to study yet.

    B) Yes, they have academic fields that interest me.

    C) Doesn't every college have off-campus bars?

    D) I'm interested in pursuing unemployment when I graduate.

2. The beauty of the campus:

    A) Is very important to me.

    B) Isn't that important.

    C) Doesn't matter, because I plan to spend my college years in a drunken stupor.

    D) Should be like an Impressionist painting, only less blurry.

3. How far do you want to be from your parents?

    A) I would like them to be able to drive down for the weekend.

    B) The more light years away, the better.

    C) It doesn't matter—as long as they give me a month's advance notice before they visit.

    D) My parents should be able to kiss me goodnight when I've had a bad day.

4. What kind of environment best suits you?

    A) An exciting city.

    B) A rural location that smells like manure.

    C) A college town with urban and rural elements.

    D) My bed; I'm hoping to take classes online and never leave my room.

5. Politically, you would prefer a school that:
   A) Has a liberal, pin-wearing, parade-marching, protest-crazy, tree-hugging student body.
   B) Has Fox News as the official network.
   C) Has a balanced mix of conservative and liberal students.
   D) Is so apathetic most people don't know who the president is.

6. In terms of sociability, you would like a student body that:
   A) Holds frat parties in the library.
   B) Goes out only during Parents' Weekend.
   C) Works hard all week but lets loose on weekends.
   D) Enforces a group-hug policy between classes.

7. Now that you're down to your final choices, the cost of college:
   A) Is the main factor that will influence my decision.
   B) Isn't a concern, because my parents have nothing better to do with their money.
   C) Will play a role in where I go; I need to discuss it with my parents.
   D) Is ridiculous—who spends $200,000 for a few classes and some beer?

Although research and feedback from others are helpful factors in choosing a college, nothing is more important than following your gut instincts. Don't hesitate to lisaten to your intuition. If that doesn't work, type "college" into your GPS next September and go wherever it leads you.

CHAPTER 15

Paying for College Without Getting Arrested

What $200,000 will buy you:

An Aston Martin

A villa in Tuscany

A small tropical island

A degree you could create at FedEx Office

Financial aid is *the* most complicated facet of the entire college admissions process. You'll hear financial aid specialists speak endlessly about FAFSA, EFC, formulas, models, software, hardware, underwear. But there are very few people who really understand how the financial aid system works. Even financial aid officers have no idea; they just input some data in a computer, cross their fingers, and hit F11.

Most financial aid packages don't even come close to covering the full cost of attending a private four-year college. The disparity between the tuition price and what families can afford to pay is often so huge that students and parents aren't sure how to bridge the gap. This chapter will explore some strategies on how to bring the two sides a little closer together.

Filling Out the FAFSA (and You Thought a Rectal Exam Was Painful)

The FAFSA (Free Application for Federal Student Aid) is one of the most personal, invasive forms you and your parents will ever have to fill out. It's really none of FAFSA's business how much your parents make, but unfortunately Mom and Dad will be forced to divulge all of their personal financial details—their salary, assets, net worth, real estate holdings, Vegas slot machine losses, and so on. But even that might not be enough for FAFSA. Don't be surprised if the following questions appear on their forms in the near future:

How much do your parents weigh?

How often do your parents engage in intimate relations? Is the TV on in the background?

Does your father sleep with his underwear on?

What do your parents argue about? Who usually wins?

What are your parents' checking account number and ATM password? (We need this for verification purposes.)

Do your parents drive nice cars or does the phrase "crapmobile" come to mind?

If you could estimate your parents' total value of cash, savings, and checking accounts, what would that number be? Could you steal some of that money without them noticing?

Figuring Out the Financial Aid Process

To educate yourself about the financial aid process, check out www.finaid.org. **FinAid** is, hands down, the most accurate, informative, and up-to-date website about financial aid and scholarships. You'll find information on every aspect of financial aid, including student loans, definitions of important terms, avoiding common errors on applications, and saving for college, as well as jokes and anecdotes. FinAid does an incredible job of demystifying the financial aid system, making it much more comprehensible for parents and students.

To help families become savvier about the financial aid process, Kalman A. Chany, a financial aid consultant and the author of *Paying for College Without Going Broke*, offers these suggestions:

- ✔ **Start early.** Don't wait until the acceptances come in to calculate financial aid. Figure out in advance how much you'll likely receive from a particular college to avoid being blindsided by your final package. Go to www.finaid.org/calculators to calculate your EFC (expected family contribution).

- ✔ **Be a smart consumer.** Keep in mind who is giving you financial aid advice. Remember that admissions officers are salespeople, so take their advice with a *bushel* of salt. Separate the college marketing pitch from reality. Read consumer friendly publications like *Kiplinger's Personal Finance* and *Money* to educate yourself—don't rely solely on potentially biased advice from colleges or banks.

- ✔ **Have a safety school.** Just as you should have a school you're 100-percent sure will admit you, Chany suggests that you also have a financial safety school—one that your family can definitely afford.

Maximizing Your Aid Package

Michael Moskowitz, the founder and CEO of MHM Consulting, a financial aid consulting firm, has the following suggestions to help families receive as much aid as possible in their initial package.

✔ **Be aware of deadlines.** "I've seen too many people forget to send a piece of paper or mix up the deadlines of different colleges and not get the aid they needed," Michael says. He suggests that families confirm the deadlines with each school's financial aid office. "Even if you think you know, double-check," he cautions. "It's also important to follow up and make sure that the school received your forms."

✔ **Let Mom and Dad take the lead.** Michael says that although students and parents should embark on the financial aid process together, it is more incumbent on parents to take the reins. "Your kids are seventeen or eighteen years old and might not know what a tax return is," he explains. "As a parent who is most likely ultimately responsible for funding your child's education, it's up to you to take the lead in the aid process."

✔ **Get the worm.** Because colleges have a limited amount of money to distribute, financial aid is allocated on a first-come, first-served basis. Take advantage of the rolling process and get your application in early. Parents shouldn't wait until they do their taxes to fill out the FAFSA. They should approximate their tax information based on the previous year and check off the "estimated" box that indicates they have not yet filed their tax returns. Once they do complete their taxes, they can always correct the information in the FAFSA if there is a disparity between their earlier estimate and the number on their tax returns. Parents should be aware that colleges will ask for their federal return to verify the information in the FAFSA.

✔ **Be conservative with numbers.** When the FAFSA asks how much liquid cash your family has, your parents shouldn't enter the balance from their bank account right after they've been paid. The people in the Federal Student Aid office won't know that the number will significantly decrease when living expenses—clothing, mortgage, food, and so on—are taken into account. Instead, your parents should put down a conservative number that more accurately reflects how much they have *after* they've paid their bills.

✔ **Make a personal connection.** If possible, find out who is responsible for processing your financial aid forms. Try to establish a rapport with this person to make the process smoother and easier. Call or email the financial aid office with questions, then introduce yourself to your officer. Thank the officer for his or her time and ask what would be the best way for you to get in touch if you have any more questions.

Negotiating Your Aid Package

The moment of truth is finally here: Your financial aid package arrives and . . . your heart sinks. Even with loans, work-study, and meager grants, you still can't cover the full cost of tuition. Not to worry. The initial aid package isn't necessary your final one—in some cases, it's negotiable and just the opening offer. Plus, financial aid officers often have a few solid suggestions to help you make up for the shortfall:

Soak your rich grandfather's dentures in liquid Drano.

Panhandle on weekends.

Save 1-900 phone calls for special occasions.

Sell your parents' house and live in the family station wagon.

When it comes to financial aid, don't expect generosity. Think of college as your tightwad uncle who has millions of dollars under his pillow yet still sends you a birthday check for $12 every year. Colleges' aid packages often run the gamut—some offer less money than what's in your piggy bank, and some offer less than what's underneath your couch cushions. In other words, most students are unpleasantly surprised when they receive their aid package. Once the initial shock wears off, you'll need to do a few things:

- ✔ **Take a deep breath.** First and foremost, try to remain calm. Remember that work-study money will kick in *after* the tuition bill is paid.

- ✔ **Do your own calculations.** Ignore how much the college says your family can contribute—you and your parents should figure out a realistic amount. Sure, Emory claims you can contribute $25,000 a year, but did they realize that doing so will force your family to move into a pueblo hut?

- ✔ **Tell your parents to be realistic with you.** Most parents hate the idea of disappointing their children, especially if they have their heart set on a certain school. But sometimes a little disappointment on your part is better than forcing your family into insurmountable debt. It's important to understand where your parents are coming from financially. Do not blame them for not having enough money to cover the full cost of tuition, at either a state or private school. You can, however, refer to them as Failure #1 and Failure #2 instead of Mom and Dad.

- ✔ **Get the details.** If you have questions about the types of loans you've been offered or want a more in-depth explanation of a college's package, call a financial aid officer at the school or make an in-person appointment, if possible. If you have questions about your sanity slowly slipping away, call your pharmacist.

- ✔ **Haggle, Middle Eastern–style.** If the University of Southern California offers you $15,000 a year and NYU offers you nothing, let NYU know. Unfortunately, the level of aid often reflects the degree to which a college wants you. If NYU wants you to attend, they will make it worth your while to do so.

✔ **Invent a family tragedy.** Just kidding—there's no way you'd get away with it. However, if your circumstances *have* changed considerably since you applied for aid (Mom was laid off, your parents got divorced, Dad lost a major asset, your aunt underwent an operation and is now your uncle), let the financial aid office know.

✔ **Write the admissions committee.** If you *really* want to attend a school that's just too costly even with aid, write an eloquent letter to the admissions committee. Don't beg, but make them aware of how much you would love to attend. Admissions officers will sometimes convince the financial aid office to change your package. It's a long shot, but it just might pay off.

Dealing with Loans, Debt, and Other Depressing Topics

loan | lōn | *n* : a crushing, oppressive weight that withers the very spirit of the person attached to it; a good way to ruin a buzz.

debt | det | *n* : the reason for taking a soulless, life-sucking, Excel-driven job after college; the motive for moving into parents' garage after graduation.

You're only eighteen—aren't you a little young to be thinking about the tens of thousands of dollars you may need to repay after college? Unfortunately, now *is* the time you have to make some serious financial decisions.

If your parents can afford the full cost of college, stop reading this chapter. (Hopefully, you'll spill coffee on your brand-new laptop.) If, on the other hand, your parents are like most people—hardworking but still overwhelmed by the astronomical cost of college—then you have a few things to consider.

1. How badly do you want to attend your first-choice college? Is it worth assuming the burden of student loans? Right now it may seem like paying them off is something you'll deal with in the far-off future, but trust me, these four years will fly. Do you want to be saddled with enormous debt after college?

2. Is there a cheaper college alternative that you can live with? Maybe a state school, which isn't your first choice, is more affordable.

If your priority is attending your top school, even if you can't afford it, then the trade-off of assuming debt is worth it. Alternatively, if you choose a more affordable school to maintain your peace of mind, then the trade-off of sacrificing your first-choice college is worth it. There's no right or wrong decision. You just need to put things in perspective and consider which factors are most important to you.

David, a high school senior from Westchester County, New York, got into Brandeis University but knew that he would be at least $100,000 in debt after graduation. He also received a full, four-year scholarship to a state school. He had a very tough choice to make. "I really wanted to go to Brandeis, but I wasn't sure if I wanted to owe so much money after college," he says. "But I was not happy at the idea of going to the state school." David decided that college was a once-in-a-lifetime experience that he didn't want to compromise by going to a school he was unenthusiastic about. He chose Brandeis.

Asha, a high school senior from Queens, New York, had a similar dilemma. She always thought the University of Pennsylvania was her first-choice school, but after receiving a full, four-year scholarship to a lesser-known university, she had a change of heart. "I looked at my financial aid package from Penn and basically had a panic attack," she says. "The other offer was too tempting to turn down."

Unfortunately, some students don't have a financially feasible college option. If you find yourself in a situation where you will be financially in the hole no matter what college you attend, don't panic. There is always a cheaper option out there: for instance, attending a two-year school and then transferring, working for a year before going to college, or paying a few hundred bucks for a bogus online degree.

Investigating Scholarships

scholarship | skä-lər-ship | *n* : a fictional term created by the same person who came up with *unicorn*.

For most students, college scholarships are very difficult to obtain. If you meet any of the following criteria, you might qualify for one:

> You are a direct descendent of the Druids of Stonehenge.
>
> You are half Cherokee, half Nigerian, half Zoroastrian, and play the didgeridoo.
>
> You plan to study the variability of mutation in polylogarithmic time.
>
> You have a birthmark over your right eye shaped like Lithuania.
>
> Your parents are immigrants from Georgia (no one needs to know it's the Peachtree State and not the former Soviet republic).
>
> You have won a Nobel Prize.

As one high school guidance counselor from New York City says, "It's really hard for a typical straight-A student who plays three sports to get a lot of the scholarships out there." There's a good reason most students don't receive scholarships (or at least those substantial enough to make a dent in tuition): They are truly hard to come by. That said, scholarships are out there. And often, finding out about them is a challenge. Here are some tips to help you locate scholarships:

- ✔ **Think local.** "Most scholarships are local," says a college consultant from Boston. "Students should see what is being offered in their town or community."

- ✔ **Check with your guidance counselor.** You may be eligible for scholarships awarded by your high school.

- ✔ **Research college scholarships.** Many colleges do offer their own scholarships, so it never hurts to find out about scholarship opportunities at the schools you're interested in. Some scholarships are automatically given to students who meet certain criteria; others can be found by doing a little research. Look at the school's website or ask the admissions office to learn about scholarship opportunities.

- ✔ **Ask your parents to look into scholarships at work.** Some corporations offer scholarships for children of employees, such as the "Get This Money-Sucking Burden Out of the House" scholarship for particularly talented children.

- ✔ **Visit FastWeb (www.fastweb.com).** A companion site to FinAid, FastWeb contains the most comprehensive and up-to-date scholarship database. Every college-bound student should set up a profile; it's quick and free and can potentially have huge rewards. Mark Kantrowitz, the publisher of FastWeb, advises students against paying for a fee-based scholarship site. "Don't pay money to get money," he says. FastWeb also refers visitors to a few other helpful free scholarship sites, such as NextStudent (www.nextstudent.com) and Broke Scholar (www.brokescholar.com).

✔ **Pursue the unusual.** Become left-handed, learn how to call ducks, add a few inches to your height, and create a prom dress out of duct tape to try to qualify for a few of the more unusual scholarships out there. Believe it or not, these are actual scholarships students can apply for.

Unfortunately, the truth is that even with a handful of scholarships, you will likely still have to pay an enormous amount of tuition. A $2,500 scholarship is fantastic, but when faced with an annual bill of $50,000 from a private school, it's just chump change.

The "Middle Class" Conundrum— Do We Look Like We Own a Yacht?

Many families find themselves in the following quandary: they make just enough money not to qualify for financial aid but still dilute the last of the ketchup with water to make it last a little longer. Are your parents stuck in that nebulous stratum that colleges like to dub "the middle class"? Sure, they've always provided you with the comforts in life; it just so happens that those comforts never included a private jet.

In terms of financial aid, many colleges have a tendency to lump middle-class families with those who own several residences, ski in Aspen, and begin every other sentence with "Want to hear about my hedge fund?" Michelle, a high school senior from Pennsylvania, says, "My acceptance to Tulane put my family in a very bad position. We didn't get any aid because, yes—on paper—we could do it, but my parents will barely have anything left over."

For many families who aren't awarded aid because they can technically "afford" the tuition, a host of problems arises. The cost of school may burden your parents to the degree that they can't take vacations, retire in the foreseeable future, or pay back their loan sharks. "My son feels like he's putting us in a very bad situation," says Mark, the father of a high school senior who is considering Emory. "We didn't qualify for aid, but paying the tuition bills will still be a struggle."

If you're in a similar situation, you need to talk to your parents. Have a frank discussion about how much of a toll college will take on their financial situation and lifestyle. Perhaps your parents are willing to sacrifice more for you than you realize. Or perhaps the strain will more extensive than you expected. Paying for college is an undertaking you and your parents must conquer together; to succeed, each of you must understand where the other is coming from.

Of course, there are certain indicators that your parents are struggling financially more than they're letting on. If Mom and Dad have done any of the following, they are probably going to excessive lengths to finance your higher education:

> To cool off, your parents squeeze into the freezer in the frozen food section of Whole Foods.
>
> Your mother sells her engagement ring and tattoos the word *wife* on her finger.
>
> Your parents talk to your younger siblings about the advantages of joining the army.
>
> Your parents buy an inflatable pool and charge you to go in.
>
> Your parents ask your retired grandfather if he'd consider working at McDonald's.
>
> Your father takes head shots and looks for work as a male model.
>
> Your parents tell you that your happiness is more important to them than eating on a regular basis.

Who's Paying? Reaching an Understanding with Your Parents

If paying for college is becoming an increasingly tense topic at the dinner table, don't be surprised if you receive the following letter:

Dear Child,

It has recently come to our attention that you were switched at birth in the hospital. Trust us, we are as shocked as you are. The fact that this discovery occurred immediately after the arrival of the financial aid packages is purely coincidental.

Incidentally, we are no longer responsible for funding your college career. We will now attempt to find our real child, who has hopefully received a full scholarship or works in a field where a college degree is not required (like mining or deep-frying poultry).

It's been a fun ride,
Mom and Dad

It's crucial to reach an understanding with your parents about who exactly is paying for your college education. "Some parents believe that it's not their responsibility to pay their kids' tuition bills," says Anne, a high school guidance counselor from outside of Boston. "All parents have a basic philosophy of 'How much do I owe my kid?'"

If you can get through the talk with your parents about the birds and the bees, you can get through the college payment discussion. Talk to them about how much they can afford to pay and what you are willing to do to help meet those tuition bills. "I've found that kids who came to a rock-solid financial agreement with their parents about college are the happiest students," says Anne. When her own children were accepted to colleges, Anne offered to pay half the tuition at the state schools.

"It made sense to my daughters to go to the state schools and pay half the tuition rather than go to private schools and pay the whole thing." Allison, a mother from Pennsylvania, told her children that they could go to expensive private schools for their undergraduate education but that they were on their own for graduate school.

Here are a few suggestions to help you and your parents come up with a mutually satisfying plan to finance your college education:

- ✔ If you have good grades, consider attending a lesser-known school that will offer you money or other merit-based incentives.

- ✔ Try the 50-50 plan: you pay half of the tuition and your parents pay the other half.

- ✔ Agree to take care of graduate school (if that's in your plans) entirely on your own.

- ✔ Get your parents to promise—in writing—to buy you a new car if you go to a cheaper school.

- ✔ Attend the less costly school on the condition that your parents won't call you for the next four years.

- ✔ Go to the school of your choice, but swear to eliminate the terms *nursing home* and *assisted living facility* from your vocabulary.

- ✔ Leave the country. A full education at Oxford University in England costs less than one year of tuition at most private schools in the United States. Higher education is one of the biggest rip-offs in this country. Our great-grandparents didn't come to America on really uncomfortable boats and toil for decades just so their offspring could work the night shift at White Castle to pay back their student loans.

CHAPTER 16

Taking a Gap Year: Should You Put Off Renaissance Poetry to Explore Italy on a Vespa?

Taking a year off between high school and college can be an incredibly healthy choice after twelve years of unremitting formal education. Before you jump into another four years of school, consider the possibility of doing something different for a year. Not sure whether or not you need a hiatus? There are a few clear-cut signs that you need some time off to recharge:

You feel burned out from four intense years of high school.

Your yearbook quote is, "I want to catch malaria teaching English next year."

You feel deep telling people, "I want to discover who I am."

You've been waitlisted at every school, including Bob's Auto Universe.

You're hoping to marry a rich foreigner so you don't have to go back to school.

Tales from the Gap Year

You're only eighteen once. If the idea of seeing the world is more appealing to you than taking a freshman seminar on the Biology of Birds, then apply for your passport and start packing. The so-called "gap year"—that year between high school and college—is already a well-accepted custom in the United Kingdom and becoming an increasingly popular option for American students who aren't quite ready to jump back into academic life.

"There is no way I could have handled college without taking time off," says Christopher, a recent graduate of the University of Maryland. Christopher spent his gap year teaching English in China. "It was this far-out, surreal, totally incredible experience that made me so much more self-reliant. I would recommend it to anybody." If you don't want Chinese food for breakfast, lunch, and dinner, not to worry—there are limitless options for the gap year. Most students mistakenly think that they have to do something structured via an organized program, such as the Peace Corps, AmeriCorps, or TEA (Teaching English to Australians). But this is *your* gap year—and it's up to *you* how to spend it.

Jill, a high school senior from Morristown, New Jersey, plans to take piano lessons during her gap year. She loves playing the piano and felt like she didn't have enough time to devote to it in high school. "It's not like I'll have time in college, because I'm not going to be a music major," says Jill, who will attend an Ivy League school after her gap year. Jill explains that she needed a breather after the intensity and stress of high school and the college application process. Although college administrators and gap year "consultants" claim that you should spend the time between high school and college productively, you don't have to. If you don't want to change the world or perfect an instrument, you could opt to spend September to June simply shopping at the Gap. Imagine how you could toy with people by saying, "I'm spending my gap year at the Gap." Talk about a growth experience. As long as the experience is enjoyable and fulfilling, then it's worthwhile.

Many top schools such as Princeton and Harvard actually encourage the gap year. However, the structured programs and volunteer opportunities can feel like round two of the extracurricular mania you went through to get into college in the first place. There's nothing wrong with studying art history in Paris or building homes in Costa Rica, but it's also perfectly fine to use your gap year for catching up on good books (*The Brothers Karamazov* by Dostoyevsky is a good place to start) or traveling for the sake of traveling.

Lauren from Tampa, Florida, decided to "bum around Europe" with her best friend during her gap year. She acknowledges that this sounds unfocused, but as she puts it, "Why does everything we do have to be so goal-oriented?" The girl does have a point. One could argue that there is no better education than traveling. (Don't pretend you're not jealous.)

Debbie from Teaneck, New Jersey, deferred her acceptance to the University of Pennsylvania and spent her gap year in Israel studying at a women's yeshiva. "I wasn't excited about school and felt that I needed this time to get to know Israel," she says. Debbie perfected her Hebrew, took fascinating courses, and ate a lot of falafel. "It was the best experience I ever had," she says.

Here are some more actual gap-year experiences from students across the country:

Taking a language immersion program in Barcelona

Starting a humorous blog that ranked fast-food joints and discussed healthy menu choices

Driving a pedicab in New York's Central Park

Moving to Paris to try to break into modeling

Creating an animated television series (which the student is currently trying to sell to networks)

Teaching English to local children in South Africa (this self-proclaimed "filthy rich brat" also learned how to do her laundry "without a laundry machine")

Coaching a high school varsity baseball team

The gap year is a blank canvas; you can fill it with whatever experiences you choose. Just remember to use broad brushstrokes, try bold colors, find new landscapes, and use nontoxic paint to avoid brain damage.

Getting Your Parents to Understand

"I've known since ninth grade that I wasn't going straight to college," says Evan, who attended a great private high school in New York City. Evan explained to his parents that he wanted to pursue a career in the music industry and needed time to think about achieving his goals. "I'm not ruling out college in the future, but right now I don't need a BA to do what I want to do," he says. "A lot of people I know go to college and then realize they need time off." Evan's parents weren't thrilled with the idea of a gap year, but they agreed to let their son take time off to figure things out; they are allowing him to live at home and pursue his musical dream. (Their feeling is that it's better for him to try this now than in twenty years.)

Unfortunately, not all parents are as understanding or supportive as Evan's. When Adam, a sophomore in the premed program at the University of Michigan, talked to his parents about spending a gap year in South America, they flat-out rejected the idea. "My dad thought it was a complete waste of time," he says. Adam thought that traveling around South America would leave him refreshed and energized to tackle the four daunting years of premed courses ahead of him. "It didn't make sense to my father for me to be a doctor at age twenty-seven instead of twenty-six." Although Adam is handling his workload just fine, he does have an underlying feeling of regret over a lost opportunity. Because of his heavy course load and requirements, he won't be able to study abroad during college. Adam hasn't completely given up his desire to travel, though—he's already thinking about taking some time off before med school. "I'm trying to plant the seeds now," he smiles.

It may be difficult for your parents to understand why you're not gliding along the usual trajectory from high school straight to college. Remind them that one year isn't going to throw your life off course and that you have your entire future to study, work, bring home the bacon, win the bread, and so on. Take advantage of your youth and embark on an experience that you might never have again. Based on the students I interviewed, most people who were interested in a gap year but went straight into college instead regretted not taking the time off. As someone famous once said, the greatest risk is never taking one.

Explain to your parents how you would benefit from the gap year: you'd become a more mature, independent adult, regroup after the stress of high school, partake in something unique, pursue a longtime dream or interest, and so on. If you don't know exactly what you hope to gain from the experience, just throw in the phrases "personal growth," "once-in-a-lifetime opportunity," and "legalized marijuana" whenever possible.

If your parents still don't understand why you need a mental health year, there are a few other tactics you can use to convince them to let you take the time off. Try out the following tried-and-true statements to motivate a change of heart.

Whether I'm living in a dorm or traveling, I'll still catch ringworm.

I'll pay for the trip with my Bar/Bat Mitzvah money.

I'll come back fluent in Bantu.

Shipping me off to a rice paddy plantation is cheaper than tuition.

It's a lot easier to have anonymous hook-ups in foreign countries.

When You Shouldn't Take a Gap Year

In some ways a gap year is a form of escapism, and there's nothing wrong with that. But it's not a good idea to run away from something that will be there when you get back. If you're always fighting with your boyfriend, a gap year isn't going to solve anything. If you don't get along with your mother, a gap year won't solve that problem either. To quote any movie on Lifetime, "You need to fix what's on the inside before you can fix what's on the outside." Running away from what's bothering you is only a temporary solution.

The following are *not* good reasons for wanting to take a gap year:

A strategy for college admission. Do not use the gap year as a way to make yourself more enticing to schools. Taking a year off is no guarantee that you'll gain admittance to a certain college.

Everyone else is doing it. Yes, it may seem trendy and hip to spend a year building plumbing systems in Central America, but a gap year is a big commitment. The desire to go must come from you, or you'll be miserable.

College tuition is a financial obstacle. If your family can't afford college, they probably can't afford to bankroll a year of foreign travel either. Don't plunge your parents into debt before you even enter college. If you still want to take a gap year, consider more affordable options. You can always intern at Starbucks.

Diversionary tactic. Your parents have grounded you, and you think dropping the "I'm delaying college for a year" bomb at the dinner table would be a good way to distract them.

So before you delay your college education, make sure you are taking a gap year for the right reasons. (And yes, being on the run from the FBI is considered a good reason.) You don't have to pinpoint exactly why you want to fertilize crops with animal dung in Mongolia—you just need a sincere desire to go, a healthy sense of escapism, and your parents' credit card.

Whether It's Fat or Thin, an Envelope Will Not Change Your Life

We have blown up the role of colleges to mythic proportions, expecting schools to take normal eighteen-year-olds and churn out superior products. But no school can do that. No college can forge your identity, equip you with the motivation to succeed, or give you the resilience to weather life's ups and downs. That's all up to you. Marilyn McGrath, director of undergraduate admissions at Harvard, puts it this way: "It's about what you do with what you have."

You are not defined by where you will spend the next four years of your life. The college you graduate from does not label you; your identity transcends that. Your alma mater does not dictate your fate; no school will ensure or deny you success in life. The only people who care where you went to college are those in the development office, who will hound you for donations for the rest of your life.

The world is equally ripe for Ivy League grads and state school grads—and, for that matter, anyone who wants to make something of himself or herself. Your diploma is just a rite of passage; real life begins once you realize that Yaffa blocks no longer count as furniture. And if college just isn't for you, the world is brimming with possibilities for people without an undergraduate education. The following jobs do not require a college degree:

Professional assassin

The guy who changes the light bulb at a lighthouse

Doctors (in certain countries)

Hand models

The naked cowboy in Times Square

You're Good Enough and Smart Enough— Who Cares Whether Admissions Officers Like You?

We all invest admissions officers and college officials with so much authority and power, yet we overlook the fact that these people couldn't survive without you. It's the students—and the parents' tuition checks—that keep American higher education afloat. Of course, it can be difficult to feel important and valuable when these officers tell you, "Don't set foot on our campus in September." Because you can't change the admissions system, try indulging in a few satisfying fantasies about what the admissions process *should* be like. In an ideal admissions world:

Students interview admissions officers. If they can't answer questions like "Who's the vice president of Bulgaria?" on the spot, they are zapped with a Taser.

Colleges submit a FAFSA-like questionnaire to parents, providing details about their investments, endowment, salary distribution, overall budget, and how much money they make from parking tickets on Parents' Weekend.

Every admissions officer reveals his or her SAT score.

Attractive students pay less tuition than ugly ones.

Instead of writing a five-hundred-word essay, students submit a YouTube video in which they mime why they want to attend a particular school.

Safety schools accept you just for putting the stamp in the right place on the envelope.

Rejection letters are abolished; instead, colleges send the rejected applicants a picture of a sad gorilla.

It's Your School

Regardless of where you end up, you will feel a sense of pride in your school. Get used to saying it: *my school*. Your school will be yours forever (unless of course you transfer—then you can start this nostalgic schmaltz with another college). So as soon as you send in your deposit, celebrate by buying every sweatshirt, baseball cap, and T-shirt available at the bookstore. And of course, nothing is official until you attach the college sticker to your back windshield.

I wish you the best of luck with your college experience. If you're still in the midst of the application process, remember that you *will* get through this. If you have any questions, comments, or concerns, feel free to contact me through my website, www.admissionsangst.com. Just don't expect a response.

Index

A

Acceptance letters, 159–60
ACT
  anxiety and, 68–71
  poor test takers and, 72
  preparing for, 64, 67
  proctors for, 70–71
  SAT vs., 54–57
  score reporting for, 57
  time constraint for, 62–63
  website for, 55
AdmissionsAngst.com, 53
Admissions officers
  behaviors hated by, 136–40
  behaviors loved by, 140–43
  communicating with, 137–39
  essays and, 110–11, 116
  impressing, 140–41
  language of, 34–35,
    142–43, 156
  parents and, 138
  questions for, 141–42
  stalking, 140
Admissions process
  absurdity of, 21
  fantasies about, 192–93
  learning about, 46–47
  limbo period in, 144–50

  parents' involvement in, 164
  risks and, 50
  websites on, 52–53
Alumni interviews. *See* Interviews
AP courses, 8–10
Applications. *See also* Essays;
  Recommendation letters
  errors in, 146–47
  reexamining, after mailing,
    146–47
  supplementary information
    with, 139
Athletes, 15–16

B

Brag sheets, 101–2

C

CollegeConfidential.com, 52–53
College fairs, 140
CollegeProwler.com, 167
Colleges
  community, 35–38
  foreign, 27, 183
  paying for, 27, 170–83
  prestigious, 25–26, 157–58,
    165–66
  safety, 172

selecting right, 22–35, 82–85, 161–69
  student feedback on, 166–67
  tours of, 73–81
Collegese, 34–35
Community colleges, 35–38
Community service, 11–12, 17
Competitions, academic, 6
Counseling. *See* Guidance counselors; Private counselors
Courses
  AP, 8–10
  elective, 10
  grades in, 12–14, 149

D
Debt, 176–78

E
EFC (expected family contribution), 27, 172
Electives, 10
Email, 137–38
ePrep.com, 67
Essays
  answering question for, 114
  categories of, 111–13
  importance of, 111
  message of, 116–18
  opening sentence of, 115
  parents and, 109–10
  sample effective, 118–25
  spell-checking, 147
  tips for, 107–8, 113–18
  topics for, 106, 114
Extracurricular activities, 2–4, 7–8, 101–2
Eye contact, 132

F
FAFSA (Free Application for Federal Student Aid), 171, 173
FastWeb.com, 179
FinAid.org, 27, 171–72
Financial aid
  deadlines for, 173
  FAFSA, 171, 173
  learning about, 27, 171–72
  maximizing, 172–74
  for middle-class families, 180–81
  negotiating, 174–76
  parents and, 173–74
Foreign colleges, 27, 183
FreeRice.com, 66–67

G
Gap year, 184–90
GotBrainy.com, 67
Grade grubbing, 12–14, 149
Guidance counselors
  becoming your own, 40–42
  dedicated vs. indifferent, 42–43
  ignoring, 43–44
  inadequate, 40–42
  job of, 39–40
  parents and, 45, 46–47
  private counselors vs., 48–52
  ratio of students to, 39

H
High school
  best approach to, 1, 2–3
  final semester of, 144–50
  gap year after, 184–90

I

IECA (Independent Educational
    Consultants Association), 49
Intel Science Talent Search, 6
Internet research
    on admissions process, 52–53
    on colleges, 166–67
    on test preparation, 66–67
Internships, 18–19
Interviews
    answers during, 133
    appearing interested during, 131
    asking questions during,
        132, 134
    connecting with interviewer
        during, 129–30
    eye contact during, 132
    location for, 134
    optional, 134–35
    personal matters and, 132–33
    promptness for, 128–29
    respect and, 130–31
    selling yourself during, 131
    speaking style for, 127–28
    typical questions in, 126–27

L

Leadership, 7–8
Legacy applicants, 164
Loans, 176–78

N

Number2.com, 67

O

Overachievers, 2–4, 8–10

P

Parents
    admissions officers and, 138
    advice for, 91–92

on college tours, 76–79
    communicating with, 85–89,
        94–95
    essays and, 109–10
    finances and, 173–74, 175,
        181–83
    gap year and, 187–89
    guidance counselors and, 45,
        46–47
    involvement of, 82–85, 164
    overbearing, 90–94
    private counselors and, 48
    quiz for, 92–94
Passion, importance of, 4–5
Personality, schools
        complementing, 28–30
Private counselors, 48–52

R

Recommendation letters
    effective, 105
    excessive number of, 138–39
    importance of, 96
    key components of, 98–102
    requesting, 97–98
    sample, 102–5
    selecting teachers for, 96–97
    waiving right to see, 105
Rejection, 151–60

S

Safety schools, 172
SAT
    ACT vs., 54–57
    anxiety and, 68–71
    fantasy questions for, 58–62
    poor test takers and, 72
    preparing for, 63, 64–68
    proctors for, 70–71
    score reporting for, 57